THE BEST BUDDHIST WRITING 2013

A SHAMBHALA SUN BOOK

THE BEST BUDDHIST WRITING 2013

Edited by Melvin McLeod
and the Editors of the *Shambhala Sun*

SHAMBHALA
Boston & London 2013

Shambhala Publications, Inc.
Horticultural Hall
300 Massachusetts Avenue
Boston, Massachusetts 02115
www.shambhala.com

9 8 7 6 5 4 3 2 1

First Edition
Printed in the United States of America

⊗This edition is printed on acid-free paper that meets the
American National Standards Institute z39.48 Standard.
♻This book is printed on 30% postconsumer recycled paper.
For more information please visit www.shambhala.com.
Distributed in the United States by Random House, Inc.,
and in Canada by Random House of Canada Ltd

Library of Congress Cataloging-in-Publication Data

The best Buddhist writing 2013 / edited by Melvin McLeod
and the editors of the *Shambhala Sun*.
pages   cm
ISBN 978-1-61180-069-2 (pbk.)
1. Buddhism. I. McLeod, Melvin, editor of compilation.
II. Shambhala sun.
BQ4055.B4754 2013
294.3—dc23
2012012376

Contents

Introduction

Traditionally in Buddhism, there are two ways to realize enlightenment. The first is sudden, an immediate flash of experience in which we finally see the true nature of reality. It can happen without warning or apparent cause, yet is only possible because of the years of discipline, effort, and meditation that preceded it. It can be triggered by almost anything—the sharp words of a teacher, a bird flying overhead, some surprising event that stops our mind. My favorite example is the Zen monk who walked out of his hut at night, perhaps on his way to the latrine, and stepped into a bucket. In that instant, it is said, his world fell apart. He saw the truth.

The second way is the gradual path to realization, so subtle we may not even know it's happening. Traditionally, it's said to be like taking a long walk through a heavy fog. It's not really raining, and you don't notice your clothes getting wet. But eventually you realize that you are covered with a fine dew of awakening.

Among Buddhist practitioners in the West there are surely some—maybe the lucky ones—who have experienced that sudden, transformative flash of realization. But most of us are walking through the mist on our path of dharma, not noticing how it clings to us until, to our surprise, we are changed.

Once I was talking with Mel Weitzman, Roshi, a senior student of the great Zen master Shunryu Suzuki Roshi, and I noted that many Western practitioners were getting discouraged because they felt their practice wasn't working. His retort was, "How would they know?"

Realization is mysterious, hard to define, and often contradictory. There is no easy way to tell if someone's meditation practice is "working." And what does that mean anyway, in a Buddhist context? When the goal is realization of nondual, nonconceptual nonego, our ordinary ideas of good and bad, sacred and profane, are not always the best guide. Some of the apparently clearest signs of spiritual progress, the ones that meet our conventional definitions, may actually be far away from genuine dharma.

Nonetheless I will hazard an opinion: I think Buddhist practice is really starting to work in America. I see a beautiful ripening and deepening in American Buddhism—in the teachings, the writings, the communities, and, most importantly, in the people. Over years of practice, study, and struggle, the mist of dharma has soaked into their minds, hearts, and lives. I think you will find this reflected in this year's edition of *The Best Buddhist Writing*.

Although Buddhism takes many different forms around the world, the Buddhism practiced in the West over the last fifty years has generally focused on meditation practice. This year's anthology is soaked in meditation—its wisdom, compassion, and openness.

Whether you are an experienced meditator or a beginner, you will find here an outstanding selection of meditation teachings from the different schools of Buddhism, each with its own techniques and special genius. You could start with the basics, such as Sakyong Mipham's effective "How to Meditate," or Elihu Genmyo Smith's simple but surprisingly profound instruction, "Be Still." From the precision of the Theravada tradition, Shinzen Young's "The Power of Gone" teaches us a Vipassana technique focusing on the exact moment when phenomena pass away. Insight Meditation Society founder Joseph Goldstein offers us a unique nine-minute meditation practice we can incorporate into our busy day. Zen teacher Ezra Bayda helps us to avoid some of the pitfalls that inevitably arise on the path of meditation, and Vajrayana master Tsoknyi Rinpoche teaches us powerful Dzogchen practices to discover our mind's inherent awareness and clarity.

With the clear and stable mind developed in the practice of mindfulness, meditators look deeply into the nature of reality. This is the practice of insight, through which we discover the basic truths that define Buddhist philosophy. We might discover, for instance, that our lives are marked by impermanence, suffering, and interdependence. These the Buddha called the three characteristics of experience, which Insight Meditation teacher Sylvia Boorstein frames for modern times in this anthology.

Our meditation might then lead us to the discovery of emptiness, the truth that all phenomena, including us, have no solid, continuous identity. The Buddha presented this great Mahayana doctrine in the famed *Heart Sutra*, but scholar and translator Karl Brunnhölzl says it could also be called "The Heart Attack Sutra." Shocking as the realization of emptiness is to our whole view of reality, he says, it is also the way to joy and fearlessness. Finally, Zen teacher Reb Anderson ties together the progression of the Buddha's teachings in "The Third Turning of the Wheel."

But what does all this great meditation and insight mean if it just stays on our cushion? We have to put it into practice in our lives, where it can really benefit ourselves and others. Fortunately, Buddhism offers many effective practices to help us be wise, loving, and skillful in all our relationships. One of the most comprehensive is a series of Mahayana practices called *lojong*, or mind training. These are encapsulated in fifty-nine pithy slogans, which the Vajrayana teacher Judy Lief shows us how to apply in our modern lives.

The Tibetan master Shyalpa Tenzin Rinpoche teaches us how we can see all our troublesome thoughts as the liberating awareness they truly are. Insight teacher Phillip Moffitt offers techniques to transform emotional chaos into confidence and clarity. And of course, the beloved American nun Pema Chödrön always has profound and practical advice for us. In this volume, she teaches us about "Living Beautifully with Uncertainty and Change."

Meditation can transform our minds, our hearts, and our lives. But it doesn't stop there. It can't. The challenges humanity faces call for deep transformation, the kind that only comes from genuine spiritual practice. People around the world must find that within their own religion or belief system, but the wisdom of Buddhist practice has something important to offer the globe. His Holiness the Dalai Lama, perhaps the world's most beloved leader, proves that, and so does the great Zen teacher and founder of Engaged Buddhism Thich Nhat Hanh. In this edition of *The Best Buddhist Writing*, he offers his vision for a more enlightened—and therefore more sustainable—society. Only this kind of profound and transformative vision offers humanity a positive, long-term future.

Meditation, relationship, society—we divide it up, but it's all just life, our lives. It's the first-person stories of practitioners' lives that have always been the best part of *The Best Buddhist Writing* series for me. It's through them that we really see how this Buddhist practice is working.

On the gradual path, we don't claim perfection. We just do our best and accept our foibles with humor and love. So we have honest, wry, heartfelt stories of life and practice such as David Rynick's "This Truth Never Fails," and James Ishmael Ford's "If You're Lucky, Your Heart Will Break." We have Rachel Neumann's self-aware and helpful thoughts about listening in "Not Quite Nirvana," and Ira Sukrungruang's funny and heart-warming memoir "Playing with Buddha." In all these we find the mix of wisdom and humanness that's probably the best sign the spiritual practice is working.

To me, it all comes together in Zoketsu Norman Fischer's "Impermanence Is Buddha Nature." Here we find the integration of practice, philosophy, and real life that points to the deepening mind and opening heart of this fine Zen teacher and writer. Like other teachings and stories in this book, it offers us hope that diligent practice, maybe without great epiphanies and realizations, changes and ripens us for the better. Like life itself, it's hard work, and it's so subtle you may not even notice it, but it works. May your robe—or suit or dress—be soaked in the mist of dharma too.

It is my privilege and pleasure to edit *The Best Buddhist Writing* series. As always, I would like to express my appreciation to Beth Frankl and all my friends at Shambhala Publications, to my colleagues at the *Shambhala Sun* and *Buddhadharma* magazines, and to my partner, Pam Rubin, and our daughter, Pearl. Finally, I thank my root gurus, the late Chögyam Trungpa Rinpoche and Khenpo Tsultrim Gyamtso, and the other great Buddhist teachers whom I've had the honor to know. With your help, all of life becomes a dharma teaching.

Melvin McLeod
Editor-in-chief
The Shambhala Sun
Buddhadharma: The Practitioner's Quarterly

This Truth Never Fails

David Rynick

The text of Buddhism today is not just philosophy and age-old teachings—
although it is that, too. It is life itself, as practitioners integrate Buddhism
into modern life, and vice versa. This is true for Buddhist teachers too, who
offer us the insight they gain as they work to make their practice an
everyday reality. Zen teacher David Rynick shares wry and lyrical stories
of the insight he gains into his own foibles as he does his best to live the
dharma.

FIRST DAY BACK

Monday morning—I wake up groggy after a week's vacation. It's
only 5:30—no need to get up yet.

I doze lightly till 6:00, when the urge to pee becomes irresistible.
I shuffle to the bathroom, do my business, then slip back between
the sheets. A humid night and the warm air already feels oppressive.
There's no drifting back to sleep this morning. I lie here—at the
beginning of my day, in the middle of my life—and work with my
brain that has already begun to scan the horizon for news of trouble.
As usual, there's an abundance available.

My anxious morning mind is like a young dog out for a walk.
Every tree and every bush must be investigated to find out who's

peed there and what the news is. The objects of my worrying investigation this morning are many. The garden is running wild—so many things to be tied up or weeded or dug up and moved. The to-do list in preparation for the next retreat and the workers who may or may not be coming today to repair the newly discovered leak in the roof. Then there is my life-coaching business—do I have enough clients? Will the next workshop really happen? And I should have replaced my website years ago—I can usually ignore this undone task, but this morning I can't seem to stay away from it.

Like a kindly yet firm owner, I allow my doggy mind to sniff around and try to keep him moving. I'd prevent him from engaging in this low-class sniffing behavior if I could, but we've had that battle for years, and he (my mind) always wins. This morning, using my firmest and not-angry-at-all owner's voice, I say, "We're not going to spend ten minutes on each smell, each worrisome thought that comes by." So we explore briefly and keep moving. I notice that it's the same everywhere I look. This morning, everything I encounter is evidence of my deficiency and the impending falling-apart of my life.

But stepping back, even just a little, I admire the brilliance of this mind-state. This anxious mind manifests an unshakable confidence that what it is seeing is the Truth. No soft liberal relativism here. This part of me is sure that he's exactly right, and from this confidence, an endless creativity arises: everything that arises is used to bolster the argument. Each new observation is used to further support the perspective that the world is a worrisome place and I am deep in real Trouble now.

My strategy this morning is just trying not to get totally hooked into one problem—to keep my doggy mind moving. And while I'm still partly asleep, I scan for other ways of working with this worried mind, strategies that might be helpful. I look for images or feelings or dreams that may be lurking in the corner.

In my mind, I come across an image of my hands moving in a way that reminds me of the flow of the flood tide coming up the Medomak River of coastal Maine. While the overall direction is clear and powerful—the tide is irresistibly coming in—the movement of the water in any particular place is chaotic and turbulent. Eddies and microcurrents flow in every direction. Two months ago, I sat in my kayak near the mouth of the river. The tide was full flood, and the water beneath my boat seemed to be flowing in many directions at once. I imagined that if every current were visible, it would look like an intricate paisley pattern of interlocking curls. Floating in my kayak, I let the gentle currents push me around—spinning the boat and taking me first one direction, then the other.

For some reason, this image, this memory, is comforting to me. Maybe all these worries are just the many currents of my life. Perhaps there is a larger direction that holds it all. What if I trust the deeper flow and just allow the boat of my self to turn with the currents?

I raise my hand to my face and touch my cheek. "There, there," I say to myself. "Everything will be just fine." I'm almost surprised to feel the stubble from my beard. This scared little boy is actually a man who still needs comfort and reassurance on this first morning back in the saddle of his work life.

And I think of how much I love to ride horses—the power and beauty of their galloping aliveness.

Ah . . . the trustworthy energy of life, in all its many forms—now I remember.

PARALLEL PLAY

Since before my daughter was born in 1986, I've had a pottery studio in our house. When she was just an infant, I used to carry her down to the studio, and she would sit on my lap as we played together with the clay. (First lesson: We don't eat clay.) Later on, in high school, she learned how to throw pots on the potter's wheel, and we worked together on making lots of pots for several pottery sales to support her college expenses. We often sat at our wheels—side-by-side— throwing. She made the bowls and I made the mugs.

Yesterday, we spent the day glazing pots in preparation for two final firings and the dismantling of the studio for our upcoming move. My wife and I are heading to a new home—a sprawling building that we will be making into a Zen Buddhist temple. As my daughter and I mix the glazes and dip our pots, I am very aware that this is almost certainly our last day working together in this studio. Though the new place has room in a huge garage, it is not certain that we will ever set up a clay studio again. This awareness and these thoughts make me unbelievably sad—that kind of sadness that rises like a wave and threatens to crash over me and drag me out to sea.

Even as I struggle to keep going, I am aware that the intensity of these feelings is way out of proportion to the reality of the day. Here I am, spending time with my daughter, doing something we love, and I am lost in this deep grief. As I let myself feel this familiar despair and as I share it with my daughter, I begin to see the deeper sources of the feeling.

The truth is, I don't want anything to change.

Though I love my grown daughter and am delighted with her emerging life and adventures, some other part of me mourns for what is already past. I miss the little girl who played with me for hours—content with the silence of parallel play with clay, with paints, with whatever junk we could glue together. And leaving this house and this studio means coming to terms with the reality that that is truly already over.

So I let myself be with this sadness, the sadness of life—the truth that everything and everyone is constantly slipping through our fingers.

We can't hold on to anything, not even those we most love. Tears and sadness seem to be an appropriate response in the face of the preciousness and transience of our lives. And as I feel and share this feeling, it begins to change—just like everything else in the universe. The wave of intensity recedes. I think of a good glaze combination for the next pot. I hear the singer singing about eyelashes perfectly designed to catch sweat.

And I am here with my daughter and myself once again.

Conscious/Unconscious

The mystic poet Kabir writes: "Between the conscious and unconscious, the mind has put up a swing: all earth creatures, even the supernovas, sway between these two trees, and it never winds down." This seems about right to me.

Yesterday I led a Zen workshop and miniretreat up in Portland, Maine. There were twelve or thirteen of us, sitting on cushions in a circle—inquiring together into this experience of being human. and in the space between us, in silence and in words, some wisdom arises—not flashy and brilliant, but perhaps more trustworthy than that. We notice firsthand the dependable miracle of the breath and experience the possibility of finding our true home right where we are—in this place, in this moment.

Leading this exploration of being alive always feels to me like a privilege. In that circle, I find words come easily—a knowing appears that I have learned to trust and follow. Sometimes the knowing disappears—and I am learning to trust and follow even that disappearing. We come together and in the meeting we see each other and are seen. Something happens beyond words.

I leave the day grateful and inspired by our work together.

Driving home, all is well until I pass through the last toll. As I slowly roll through the E-ZPass lane, the green "Thank you!" light fails to come on. I continue through anyway and reach up to check my transponder unit, which is hidden behind the rearview mirror. It's not there.

In an instant, I realize it is in our other car and I have just driven illegally through six tolls in three different states.

I am deeply chagrined. Where has all my wonderful Zen mindfulness and equanimity suddenly gone? I am now a guilty man, an outlaw. I want to turn myself in and pay the tolls, but I am not sure how to do it. Will they even notice? Will I have to pay big fines for my mindlessness? Will the state police be waiting at my door when I return home? The ruminating mind appears and keeps me company for the rest of my trip. Swinging between the two trees of conscious and unconscious. So it goes. So we go. And maybe none of it is a problem to be fixed—just the sea waves of my life running up the inclined beach and falling back only to gather and return once more.

Be Still

Elihu Genmyo Smith

It is the most radical thing we can do: nothing. To sit down, slow down,
and finally stop—it's counter to everything we're taught life is about. And
that's the point. Being still is the antidote to this wheel of suffering that
Buddhism calls samsara. Here's Zen teacher Elihu Genmyo Smith on
this unnatural yet most natural act.

Sitting is a natural slowing down of this rushing, self-centered, mind-body chattering that we often live. This is the practice of realization, which is what we are, and this practice allows us to be who we are. As we practice, we discover who and what we are. This is the process of sitting, whether for one period or for many years.

My dharma teacher, Charlotte Joko Beck, often quoted an expression from the Hebrew Bible: "Be still, know I am." In a way, this expression clarifies and reflects realization practice; this being still is our practice, our zazen practice, our life practice. The truth of our life is that we are still, that we "know I am." Being still is not a means to an end; it is not that we should be still and then create something else or change. Being still is being who we are.

This might seem like a means-end process to us because we tend to see and understand our life in terms of a dualistic perspective; we tend to understand our life as self and not self, as before and after, as made of specific conditions. From that perspective and perception, we misconstrue who and what we are, and therefore rush around in all sorts of self-centered ways to deal with our fear in the midst of this impermanence, in the midst of this ongoing change that is being still, that is this unborn, that is this undying.

We try to do something to avoid the pain that we think is here, which is caused by our belief that we are dualistic, that we are self and not-self. So be still, be the stillness that you are; see that this is the practice. Suzuki Roshi used to say, "You are perfect as you are, and you can use some improvement." Improvement is your practice-effort in the midst of the perfection that we are. Perfection perfecting perfection.

Many teachers have their own expressions. Maezumi Roshi used to say, "Appreciate your life." Not change your life, not make your life more like it should be, but appreciate your life; appreciate this opportunity in the midst of the perfection that you are. Appreciation is your practice. In the midst of the stillness that you are, practice manifests as this life.

This is what we are doing. We get to notice this, maybe just a little bit, as we settle into zazen and into this moment. In a way, the forms and schedule of practice force us to settle, despite our wanting to rush around inside and outside; it forces us because we are this body-mind moment. Sitting still, settling our self into this moment, settling our self onto our self, settling "into" this that we are—that is what zazen is. We have the choice to settle where we are or to refuse to be where we are. Of course, we don't go anywhere else, but if we refuse to be where we are, we miss this life that we are. Instead, we can settle in the midst of ongoing change.

We are change itself. We often think of our life in terms of things changing: we like some changes and we don't like others; we want things to change in some ways and not in other ways. And of course, this moment of ongoing change is our opportunity for skillful, appropriate responses to the circumstances that reveal themselves, the conditions that reveal themselves as this moment. And yet, we are change itself. The Sixth Ancestor of Zen said, "Ongoing change is buddhanature." We are buddhanature itself, if I can say this in such a way. And buddhanature itself is the opportunity to be still, to be this that we are, to know this that we are. Stillness is ongoing change; they are not two different things.

"Be still, know I am" is not talking about knowing conceptually. This knowing is a knowing of not-knowing; this knowing is the deep *prajnaparamita* (perfection of wisdom) of the *Heart Sutra*, which says, "Avalokiteshvara Bodhisattva doing/being deep *prajnaparamita.*" You all know very well that Avalokiteshvara isn't someone else. Being this wisdom that you are, you can see the emptiness of all the five conditions, you can see the boundlessness of the ongoing change that you are, and thus you can relieve suffering and pain. What suffering and pain? The suffering and pain that come from misperceiving, misunderstanding, and mistaking our self to be a duality of self and not-self.

As we live this practice life, we have little glimmers of this truth that we are. We have glimmers not because things change but because all of a sudden we see right where we are. We see being just this moment, and we see that we can manifest this compassion that we are—this compassion naturally comes forth in being just this moment.

To say it differently, being still is being this life as it is right now, which reveals this not-two. Of course, if we are just saying "not-two" or "nondual," these are just more words. We could say what is so; we could reveal what is so. Even that is just candy; it is just encouragement for us "to do," because by doing, we see and we are. We have to do our part, despite the fact that we are perfect as we are; we have to do our part, despite the fact that from the beginning we are this realized life. Yet because we are such, we can be such. Or to add the imperative: "Because you are such, hurry up and be such a person."

Because you are stillness, be stillness. This is really what we are doing here: you are allowing yourself to be who and what you are at this moment. We are being seamless; we are living a seamless life, a shadowless life.

Now remember, I write these words not because you have to

agree or figure them out but rather to encourage us to do what we each can do as our own life. Because we each have this capacity to be seamless; we each have this capacity because this is who we are. We have this capacity in this breath, in this body-mind moment. So we don't have to add anything extra; we can simply allow ourselves to be right where we are.

The Buddha Walks into a Bar

Lodro Rinzler

Lodro Rinzler is one of Buddhism's new young voices. He's funny, Brooklyn-hip, and, in spite of his Tibetan first name, quintessentially American. Despite the catchy title of his book—The Buddha Walks into a Bar—he teaches a meditation practice that is beyond trendiness, beyond generations, beyond time and culture altogether.

When I was young I had an alarm clock shaped like a Japanese samurai, with a sword in his hand and a clock in his belly. For the ten years it worked, I would wake up every morning with the sound of a warrior yelling in Japanese, "Wake up! Wake up! It is time for the battle!"

For many of us, life does feel like a battle. Our first instinct in the morning is one of self-protection, wanting to burrow back under the covers instead of facing the day. This is because we often view our daily routine as just a way to get by in life—pay the bills, find a romantic relationship, maintain our friendships, nurture our family life—and at the end of the day we are exhausted by our struggle to keep it all together.

We spend so much energy constantly trying to keep up with

voice mail, e-mail, junk mail, bill mail, females, or males. Instead of engaging these various aspects of our life with an open mind, we schlep our way through them and cling to our escapes: we chew our nails, drink beer, have sex, shop online, or go to the gym. Some of us might even be able to multitask and do all of the above at once. Although we try our hardest, we know that at the end of the day there is always another thing we should do, and yet we have taken so little time to take care of ourselves.

This is when meditation is especially useful. Meditation practice is first and foremost about learning to be present and appreciate the world around us. It helps us view the world not as a battlefield, but as fertile ground to practice being openhearted and awake. Buddhist teachings show us that the only thing keeping us from being truly present with our world is a strong hang-up on our habitual way of looking at things.

Most of us have a set routine that gets us through our day. Somewhere along the line, we solidified that routine into a way of life. The question then becomes, "Is it working?" Day by day, we may find ourselves getting restless with the same classes or job, the same relationship, the same hangouts or hang-ups, and we long for some radical change.

However, it is not our world that is necessarily problematic; it's our point of view. It has been said that enlightenment is merely things as they are before we color them with our hopes and fears. If we could relax our idea of the way things should be and appreciate them as they are, then the world would be magically transformed into a rich ground of possibilities.

In the years I have been teaching Buddhism, I have often been struck by the incredible diversity in the sort of people who show up on the doorstep of meditation centers. Despite race, age, or economic class, the one unifying factor seems to be that none of them are entirely satisfied with their lives as they currently stand. More often than not, they have tried everything else to make life more fulfilling— the new drug, the new job, the new car, the new romance—and yet none of it has brought a happily-ever-after scenario.

The Buddhist word for the cycle of suffering we find ourselves in is *samsara*. Samsara is everything from being uncomfortable because you have a hangnail, all the way to losing a beloved friend or family member. It is the fact that we long for what we don't have, and that makes us unhappy. It is the fact that when we get what we longed for, we're already thinking about something new that could entertain us.

Samsara is fueled by hope and fear. We hope we will do well at work, but fear we'll upset our boss. We hope to go to the beach, but fear rain. Extreme hope and fear can sometimes ruin an experience because we have spent so much time in our head agonizing over what could possibly happen. Having acknowledged that external factors may not bring lasting happiness, most people are inspired to look within for change, but most of us have no idea how to begin.

This general dissatisfaction is what the Buddha taught about when he opened his mouth for his first sermon ever. He didn't say, "Here's the plan, guys. Do X, Y, and Z, and you too will glow just like me." Instead he said, "Listen. You guys are unhappy, right? Let's analyze that." He then went on to point out that we suffer because we don't know much about who we are. The good news is that he said there can be a cessation to this whole restless-life syndrome and he laid out a path for us to explore ourselves and find our own way to awakening the heart and mind. That path is one of meditation and good conduct.

Meditation is a simple tool for self-reflection, yet it has tremendous power. While it does not offer you the cure-all to transform your life, meditation definitely has the power to transform your mind and heart, making them more expansive and more able to accommodate the obstacles you face on a daily basis. The more expansive your mind and heart, the more you are able to engage your world without life feeling like a battle.

There are three stages people go through as they enter into meditation practice. The first one could be described as the "Where did all these thoughts come from?" phase. We are so used to our hectic way of life that the simple act of sitting down to meditate and being present with our breath shows us that a waterfall of thoughts is pouring through us at light speed. We have never taken the time before to look inward, and it is shocking to find the quickly shifting tones of passion, anger, confusion, loneliness, and multiple variations thereof going through our head.

The basic technique of meditation is to take an upright posture, connect with our body, and focus our mind on the breath. The breath serves as an anchor, lodging us in this very moment, the present experience. That sounds simple enough, but after a few moments we begin to notice our mind drifting off to a conversation we had earlier that day, or forming a checklist of things we need to do the moment we are done meditating. When these thoughts come up, we are instructed to acknowledge them, not as good or bad, but just as thoughts, and bring our attention back to the physical sensation of the breath. If it is helpful, we can even mentally say "thinking" to ourselves in order to acknowledge that we are not doing anything horrible, and that we have the ability to return to the breath.

In one half-hour meditation session, we could have a wide variety of thoughts. Often in the "Where did all these thoughts come from?" phase, people get frustrated because they feel like they are not getting anywhere or that meditation does not work for them. Meditation has worked for numerous average-Joes-turned-meditation-masters over thousands of years, but you, you're most likely hopeless, right?

One of the beautiful things about Buddhism is that it does not worship Buddha as a god or deity, but instead celebrates the Buddha as an example of a normal person like you and me who applied a good deal of discipline and gentleness to his meditation practice, and ended up opening his mind and heart in a very big way.

When the Buddha was in his twenties, he wasn't some great enlightened master. His name was Siddhartha Gautama, and he lived at home with his father. He had a wife that he married at an early age, and before he knew it they had a son. He was also just discovering how sheltered he had been growing up, because it was only in his twenties that he first encountered suffering in the form of sickness, old age, and death. Not unlike most of us in our twenties, he didn't like what he saw in the world, and endeavored to find a way to change it.

Siddhartha Gautama, who I imagine was known as "Sid" by close friends and family, was inspired to pursue a spiritual life away from home. He went to great extremes to starve himself and live in harsh conditions in the name of holiness, as if he wanted a radical change from his cushy upbringing. Ultimately he discovered that by not being too indulgent or too hard on himself, he could tread a middle way where he could be kind to himself, practice meditation diligently, and live a noble life. Only then was he able to attain enlightenment.

Whenever people in the "Where did all these thoughts come from?" phase ask me what to do about their meditation practice, I recall what my teachers have told me: "Keep sitting." This is not some trip about having faith because a guy named Sid did it twenty-six hundred years ago, or because we can turn to people within meditation communities and see that others have benefited greatly from this practice. It is because we can see the effects of meditation ourselves.

When the Buddha attained enlightenment, he sought out close friends who had meditated with him in the past. Instead of approaching them with the mentality of "I've figured it out, now come study with me," he simply said, "Come and see for yourself."

Meditation is a path of self-discovery. If we take the advice of the Buddha and other great teachers from the past and continue to practice meditation, we too begin to move away from feeling like we are being bombarded by a waterfall of thoughts. Instead, it may feel more like we are in the midst of a very powerful thought river. This is not a bad start. Over time and with practice, it feels like the thoughts bombarding us are more at the pace of a babbling brook or gentle stream, which ultimately leads to the mind of wakefulness—a large spacious pond without a ripple on it.

The gradual process of getting accustomed to returning to our breath during meditation practice begins to develop some mental space, which over time, without us having to "do" anything at all, naturally begins to manifest in our daily life. In our meditation practice, we learn to acknowledge our thoughts without acting on them. This is an incredibly helpful tool when we live in a world where one angry e-mail or one delete button on a cell phone can end a relationship.

Perhaps during a meditation session we find ourselves angry with a coworker or classmate. We run through a number of pretend conversations with this person and tell them off in a different way each time. We analyze exactly how they wronged us in the past, and think of how we could get even. Each time we catch ourselves doing this during our meditation practice, we acknowledge it, label it "thinking," and return to the breath. It may run something like this:

"Brett is a real asshole."

"Thinking." Back to the breath.

"Brett really went out of his way to ruin my morning, didn't he? I bet he planned to—"

"Thinking." Back to the breath.

By repeating this simple practice of allowing space on the meditation cushion, we are preparing to relate to this emotion and this person in our daily life. It is called "meditation practice" because we are practicing being present with our experience during meditation, and this practice spills over into the twenty-three-and-a-half hours we are not formally meditating. Hopefully, the next time we see Brett, instead of buying into our habitual response of lashing out at him, we will encounter a small gap of spaciousness, a chance not to react as we always have in the past, and we will be able to just be present with whatever situation arises.

When we have such an experience, we may have graduated to the second phase, the "This thing actually helps me a little" phase. We are slightly tickled that meditation is starting to allow us to access more expansiveness in our mind and daily life. This is because meditation practice is not about trying to live up to some ideal version of who we are, but instead is about just being with ourselves and our experience, whatever it may be.

The third phase can be referred to as the "Meditation is like crack" phase. We have seen that by creating a more spacious situation around the thoughts and strong emotions affecting us in our meditation practice, we are more available to relate to them fully in our daily life. That feels good. So good that we want to continue to explore this path in the hope that we can bring some sense of sanity to ourselves, our daily life, and the world around us.

However, just like it took our prime example the Buddha many years to find a technique that worked for him, we cannot expect meditation to change our life overnight. If you want to get your body in shape, you don't expect a radical difference after a few days of running or a long weekend at the gym. Instead you start off slowly by getting accustomed to the weights and machines, building your strength session by session over a good deal of time. You feel inspired each time you are able to push yourself just a little more.

The same rule applies to our mind in meditation. We cannot expect to sit down for five hours and get enlightened. Nor should we sit fifteen minutes a day for a week, and when we feel that we are no more sane or openhearted than before, give up. Session by session, we begin to build up the mental flexibility and openness that make our mind hearty and strong. We need to start by training our mind regularly in short sessions, in order to build up the stability that eventually spills over into the rest of our lives.

Ultimately I believe that anyone attracted to a spiritual life wants to be of benefit to the world. No one starts to meditate because they want a better car or better-looking partner. We want to learn how to be sane, how to be more openhearted in our daily lives, and how to spread sanity and compassion in an increasingly chaotic world. The first step is encountering our mental demons through getting to know ourselves in meditation. We need to befriend ourselves, and as clichéd as it sounds, love ourselves, so that we can be available to love the world.

The samurai alarm clock points to one way we can approach our day. Every morning we can wake up and think, "It's time for the battle. Me versus the world." In order to win, we can be ruthless at work and get raises and promotions, buy the hottest new gadgets, and have a supermodel spouse. That point of view gets old and exhausting, because we are constantly struggling to reach that new rung on the ladder of our career, our gadgets are outdated in months, and our partner's looks ultimately fade. Viewing our day as a battle separates us from the world around us and makes it appear that our daily lives are something that we need to conquer, subjugate, or just survive.

Instead you can view your life as a rich opportunity. When the alarm clock goes off, you can take a minute to reflect on everything you have in your life—your friends, family, whatever you care about—and appreciate it. As you enter your day, you could take some time to meditate, and watch how taking that little bit of time for you makes you feel more spacious and your mind more expansive.

If you do this, you may find that the world that previously seemed so intimidating, so worth fighting against, is not as difficult when you don't bring your fixed passion, aggression, and confusion to each scenario, and instead infuse each new situation with spaciousness. The less we buy into our set version of how things should be, the more we can be available to things as they are. When we are able to do this, our lives are not a battle, but a playground for us to enjoy.

How to Meditate

Sakyong Mipham

Buddhists have been studying the mind for thousands of years—and studying the best ways to study the mind. They have developed clear and practical systems to tame our mind, techniques that engage all aspects of our being. In his new book, Running with the Mind of Meditation, *Sakyong Mipham shows us how mind, breath, and energy work together in meditation to transform our lives.*

When I was trained in meditation as a child, I was asked to sit there and follow my breath for an hour. I found my mind darting from one thought to another. The act of paying attention to the breathing and following it seemed quite arduous. In a very basic way, I was not in shape. My mind did not have the strength to hold what I was focusing on for more than a few moments. But after a short amount of practice, I was able to find my breath in minutes—and follow it.

Through my continued training, I have used a wide range of meditative techniques—from the simple stabilization of focusing the mind, to visualization, to contemplative meditation, to the use of mantras. All these depend on developing some basic aspects of mindfulness, which we could equate with strength training, and awareness, which we could equate with flexibility, endurance, and stamina.

One of the most basic and helpful meditative techniques essentially consists of paying attention to the breathing. This is often called following the breath, or mindful breathing. It leads to peaceful abiding.

To train in this technique, first take the appropriate posture. Sit still, in an upright and comfortable way. Whether you are sitting on a cushion or on a chair, hold your spine upright, with a natural curve. Rest your hands on the thighs, with arms and shoulders relaxed. The chin is slightly tucked in, and the eyelids are half-shut. Relax your face and jaw. The eyelids are relaxed. The tongue is also relaxed, the tip resting against your upper teeth. Your mouth is ever so slightly open. If you're sitting on a cushion, keep your ankles loosely crossed. If you're sitting on a chair, keep both feet firmly on the floor. Rest your gaze roughly six feet in front of you.

Now take your mind away from its current thought or worry and decisively place your attention on the breathing. This is known as placement, the first of nine stages in the process of strengthening and developing the mind. These are placement, continuous placement, repeated placement, close placement, taming, pacifying, thoroughly pacified, one-pointed, and equanimity. The first three stages are connected with stabilizing the mind.

Because we have not worked with the mind before, our first experience is that it is continually moving. The mind is perpetually flooded with thoughts. This stage is likened to a waterfall; the mind feels like a torrent of water.

Initially, it is important not to feel overwhelmed or disheartened by the influx of thoughts, simply recognizing just how many thoughts are coming into our mind. As we continuously and repeatedly place the attention back on the breathing, the mind becomes stronger and stronger. It's like doing repetitions in the weight room.

The breath itself is rhythmical, soft, consistent, and soothing. By meditating upon the breath, we are getting used to the breath. Through that familiarization, the mind is now absorbing positive and helpful qualities.

Next we follow one cycle of breathing. This is ordinary breathing; nothing is exaggerated. The breath leaves the lips and nostrils. It dissolves at about six feet in front. At the end of the breath, there is a slight pause, a slight openness. Then we begin to follow the breathing cycle back to the lips.

By placing the mind on the breath, we are practicing mindfulness. We are strengthening our mind, building the base. With this seemingly simple technique, our attention is becoming stronger. Plus we are not thinking about other things, so naturally there is peace, which is very helpful for the mind.

After you do this for a few cycles, you may lose your mindfulness and instead chase thoughts about what happened that day. So the next thing you practice is not being distracted by thoughts. This takes awareness. It does not really matter what kind of thoughts you are having. When you become aware that you are thinking, simply acknowledge that you are thinking and bring your attention back to your breath. You can say to yourself, "Not now, thoughts," or remind yourself, "Oh, I was thinking." Don't feel bad; just return to the breath as quickly and simply as you can. This is how to train in the stages of placement, continuous placement, and repeated placement.

Try to gently and firmly keep your mind on the breathing. When you are aware that you are thinking, remind yourself to come back to the breath. Taking your attention away from thoughts and placing it on the breath is the focus of meditation, which in this simple form is simply the process of being mindful of the breathing, being aware that you are thinking, and returning your attention to the breath.

As we continuously and repeatedly reassociate the mind with the breathing, we are creating stability. This fourth stage—being able to keep the mind on the breath without distraction—is called close placement. Our meditation is stable, and our mind is slowly being tamed. This is how we establish a base in meditation training. When we've established the ability to pay attention to the breath, our ability to focus on any other object or endeavor is strengthened.

In the meditation tradition, the mind is considered to be located in the head, the heart, and throughout the body. However, mind and body are ultimately a single entity. This is the feeling of unity, oneness, or centeredness.

In particular, there is said to be a unique relationship between the breath and the mind. In Tibet, we say that the breath is like a horse, and the mind is like the rider. When the breath is calm and in control, it is much easier to access the mind. The Tibetan word for breath, or wind, is *lung*. This wind represents movement and energy throughout the body.

A heightened thought process such as worry increases the movement of wind. The more erratic the wind, the more it moves throughout the body. We experience it as agitated, discursive thinking and emotional highs and lows, which translate into stress— blocked energy. When we run, that wind begins to settle down, and the blockages begin to clear.

In Tibet, we have a traditional image, the windhorse, which represents a balanced relationship between the wind and the mind. The horse represents wind and movement. On its saddle rides a precious jewel. That jewel is our mind.

A jewel is a stone that is clear and reflects light. There is a solid, earthly element to it. You can pick it up in your hand, and at the same time you can see through it. These qualities represent the mind: it is both tangible and translucent. The mind is capable of the highest wisdom. It can experience love and compassion, as well as anger. It can understand history, philosophy, and mathematics— and also remember what's on the grocery list. The mind is truly like a wish-fulfilling jewel.

The reason the windhorse carries this jewel is that the mind itself is carried by wind. With an untrained mind, the thought process is said to be like a wild and blind horse: erratic and out of control. We experience the mind as moving all the time—suddenly darting off, thinking about one thing and another, being happy, being sad. If we haven't trained our mind, the wild horse takes us wherever it wants to go. It's not carrying a jewel on its back—it's carrying an impaired rider. That horse itself is crazy, so it is quite a bizarre scene.

By observing our own mind in meditation, we can see this dynamic at work.

Especially in the beginning stages of meditation, we find it extremely challenging to control our mind. Even if we wish to control it, we have very little power to do so, like the infirm rider. We want to focus on the breathing, but the mind keeps darting off unexpectedly. That is the wild horse. The process of meditation is taming the horse so that it is in our control, while making the mind an expert rider.

It is common to imagine that in meditation we are not supposed to think. That is somewhat inaccurate. What is really happening in meditation is that we are developing the ability to think when we want to, and to not think when we don't want to. We're developing the ability to direct our thoughts and focus them on the object of our choosing. For example, if we want to develop compassion, we practice focusing on thoughts of compassion, or on thoughts of people who move us toward compassion. If instead we find ourselves thinking about ice cream, and then about how our mother used to bake cookies, we are back on the wild horse. We did not intend to think those thoughts. When the mind is running everywhere, it is less available, and we feel tired, heavy, and stressed.

It's true that in the beginning stages of meditation, we want to avoid too much thinking. At that point, thinking just stimulates the wind, which we experience as discursiveness. Therefore the way to train the horse at every stage is to bring the mind back to what we want to focus on. In the beginning, we want to focus on the breathing.

By following the breath and beginning to pace the breath, we develop a steady, rhythmical flow, out and in. This flow calms the mind, which is like training the horse. Every time the horse wants to leave the trail because it sees some nice morsel of grass—be it a random discursive thought or a large fantasy—we bring the horse back to the trail. In this case, the trail is the breath.

Where the Heart Beats

Kay Larson

When did Buddhism—the real thing—come to the West? History tells
us of a few beautiful moments of transmission, when Buddhist mind and
American mind first connected, and genuine dharma was born on Western
soil. One of the earliest and most important was a series of seminars on
Buddhist philosophy taught at Columbia University by the Japanese Zen
scholar and writer D. T. Suzuki. Among the important American artists
and intellectuals who attended was the avant-garde composer John Cage.
As Kay Larson tells us in this fascinating history, Cage's famed 4'33",
known unofficially as "the silent piece," stopped the mind of American
cultural aficionados, as any great koan should.

It's the end of August, 1952. Carolyn and Earle Brown, John Cage,
David Tudor, and M. C. Richards are all driving up the Hudson Val-
ley together, headed to the little Catskills art colony of Woodstock.
The Browns have just moved to Manhattan, and already they're on
an adventure. Cage carries a new score, which will prove to be his
most notorious, most perplexing creation. The turning moment of
silence in the American arts is about to be given its debut.

Tudor is on the bill as the featured pianist at the Maverick Concert Hall, in a benefit sponsored by the Woodstock Artists Associa-

tion for its Artists Welfare Fund. The Maverick is a drafty, hand-built barn—a "rustic music chapel"—built on the property of turn-of-the-century novelist and poet Hervey White.

Maverick concerts in the early 1950s drew a clique of traditional musicians. Among them was the composer and concert violinist William Kroll, who founded the Kroll Quartet, taught in New York and Baltimore, and divided his summers between Woodstock, New York, and Tanglewood, in the Berkshires of Massachusetts, where he was director of the chamber music series. Leon Barzin, another local luminary, pulled weight as conductor, violinist, and musical director of the National Orchestral Association and the New York City Ballet.

In 1952, Maverick had its own Society for New Music, at which all the same names repeat. Maverick audiences were drawn from an equally small pool; new faces were rare enough to occasion a comment in the local press.

Into this tempest-tossed teapot came John Cage.

The Performance

Carolyn, Earle, M. C., and John settle onto hard wooden benches and chairs in the Maverick. Behind them, the gambrel roof of the barn holds an arch of old window sashes, a homegrown Woodstock version of a cathedral's stained-glass rose window. In front of them is a small, shin-high stage, low enough so a performer can step up in one hop.

Outside, the soft gray sky is sultry and threatening rain. Peeking at the program, the audience can see Cage's music listed twice. The first piece of the evening is identified simply by the date. Later titled *Water Music*—a first cousin of *Water Walk*—it's scored for such noisemakers as a duck call, three whistles, a deck of cards, water gurgling from containers, a radio, and a stopwatch. (Cage has already presented this piece at the New School for Social Research in May and at Black Mountain College on August 12.)

Just before Henry Cowell's *The Banshee,* the program lists a second work by Cage.

To play it, Tudor sits at the piano, sets out a stopwatch, carefully closes the keyboard lid, studies the score, and doesn't move for thirty seconds. He raises the lid and looks at the stopwatch.

He carefully closes the lid, studies the score, and doesn't move for two minutes and twenty-three seconds, as wind gusts through the wide-open doors at the rear of the hall and rain titters on the roof.

He raises the lid and looks at the stopwatch. He carefully closes the lid, studies the score, and doesn't move for one minute and forty seconds, while people mutter and rustle in their seats. Then he stands up and walks off stage.

Cage dryly observes the interesting sounds people make as they walk out of the hall.

That's it. Not much, right?

Then the aftermath begins. And it has proved momentous.

THE WRATH OF THE SCORNED

The furor that arose around *4′33″* inflamed the town for weeks afterward. The anger was so great, Cage observed, that he lost friends. "They missed the point," he said. "There is no such thing as silence."

Eleven days later, on October 9, a letter scorched the pages of a now-defunct local newspaper. The writer chose to be anonymous, and was identified only as "an internationally known musician, composer, and conductor." The newspaper clipping betrays the fury of a music lover scorned:

> We had been told that Cage's show had been quite impressive in New York last winter and we were all looking forward to a stimulating evening of musical experimentation. Precedents were to be broken. The Maverick was to be alive with music on a weekday evening, the sacred hall was at last going to ring with something new. We anticipated an honest, though controversial musical adventure.

What did we get? A poorly timed comedy show with worn-out musical gags repeated over and over again, boredom extended ad infinitum, yea, ad nauseam.

The duck calls and water pitchers were bad enough, but the worst offender, *4′33″*, brought the letter writer to stuttering outrage.

This form of phony musical Dadaism built up by sensational publicity, frightens audiences away from the real music of our times. The arrogance of its nihilistic sophistries might be just amusing to most people. But there is a war of nerves against common sense today particularly in all fields of art. And if we don't check these insipid fungus growths that eat into the common sense of our people, their destructive influence will grow and gradually undermine the health and vitality of our civilization.

4′33″ EVER SINCE

Over the next half century, *4′33″* has continued to be confounding on many fronts at once. Practically everything about it—including its informal title, "the silent piece"—is contested in one way or another.

One can easily get lost in the minutiae of *4′33″*—the several scores, the differing instructions, the later versions—and miss the big issues. Cage was still trying to get the message across in 1988, four years before his death:

[Cage:] I knew that it would be taken as a joke and a renunciation of work, whereas I also knew that if it was done it would be the highest form of work. Or this form of work: an art without work. I doubt whether many people understand it yet.
[Q:] Well, the traditional understanding is that it opens you up to the sounds that exist around you and—

[Cage:] To the acceptance of anything, even when you have something as the basis. And that's how it's misunderstood.
[Q:] What's a better understanding of it?
[Cage:] It opens you up to any possibility *only* when nothing is taken as the basis. But most people don't understand that, as far as I can tell.

Stepping gingerly around the bog of interpretations, we go to Cage's Zen teacher D. T. Suzuki and ask his advice. "Properly speaking, Zen has its own field where it functions to its best advantage," he tells us at the beginning of *Third Series*. "As soon as it wanders outside this field, it loses its natural color and to that extent ceases to be itself. When it attempts to explain itself by means of a philosophical system it is no longer Zen pure and simple; it partakes of something which does not strictly belong to it."

So—let's predict—all the musicological interpretations of *4'33"* are doomed to fail. They all consist of tossing sticks (forms) into emptiness.

Then what is *4'33"*? Before anything else, it's an experience.

David Tudor walks across the stage and sits down within the boundaryless universe. He crosses his legs (so to speak) and begins an interval of non-doing.

As the stopwatch ticks, he will perform "nothing."
In these four-plus minutes an opening occurs.
No expression of will or ego.
No walls between composer and performer.
No walls between the pianist and the people listening.
No dualistic divisions into "high" or "low," "good" or "not good."
No "art" versus "life."
No value judgments and no lack of value judgments.
No arising and no lack of arising.
No separation of any kind—no walls at all—and therefore perfect interpenetration.

No form and no lack of form, no emptiness and no absence of emptiness.

No sensation and no lack of sensation.

No music and yet the music of the world.

Cage: Well, I use it constantly in my life experience. No day goes by without my making use of that piece in my life and in my work. I listen to it every day. . . .

I don't sit down to do it; I turn my attention toward it. I realize that it's going on continuously. So, more and more, my attention, as now, is on it. More than anything else, it's the source of my enjoyment of life. . . .

But the important thing, surely, about having done it, finally, is that it leads out of the world of art into the whole of life. When I write a piece, I try to write it in such a way that it won't interrupt this other piece which is already going on.

Cage had (two years earlier) decided to adopt Zen discipline in the form of chance operations. Music was silent prayer—he knew that already. For almost a decade he had been seeking the perfect vehicle. So is *4'33"* Cage's version of zazen? Okay, that's fine—but what is zazen? Crossing one's legs? Watching the breath? Saying nothing? Waiting for the bell to ring? That's where the beginner begins.

After a bit more practice, however, zazen expands.

Everything interpenetrates, right? Sitting silently, where are you? Who are you? What are you sitting within?

As you cross your legs on the cushion, singing a *dharani* of transformation, the whole world flows in and through you, and all around you. The totality of creation is sitting with you. Where are the walls? Sitting zazen, you take apart the bricks one at a time, look at them carefully, and set them down. At the end of the process, where are the walls?

Cage: [A] religious spirit in which one feels there is nothing
to which one is not related . . . This is the experience of
silence.

D. T. Suzuki's mindstream pervades this moment like a per-
fume. We notice that *4'33"* is not an *interpretation* of Suzuki's
teachings, but it *embodies* them perfectly.

In this interval of silence and non-doing, *4'33"* is always itself.

It is always wide open to everything that passes through it.

The ego-oval is emptied out to welcome the flow from all directions.

Not a single thought arises in *4'33"*.

The ego noise of the audience, on the other hand, is deafening.

The composer has not expressed anything.

Instead, he has expressed nothing.

And the "music of the world" arises from the ground that is no
ground at all—unnamed and unnameable, empty of categories, beyond anything that can be said about it—the nothing that sings.

I've seen *4'33"* in many locations and circumstances. At Carnegie
Hall in New York, the pianist Margaret Leng Tan theatrically raised
her arms over the piano keyboard. Her descending hands halted just
above the keys. The well-trained audience froze, respectfully. The
overheated room seemed to have soaked up all the music ever played
within its walls.

At the Cooper-Hewitt, National Design Museum, on Fifth Avenue, I slipped through a door into the garden. On a green lawn
enclosed by a low wall that did nothing to keep out the roar of Manhattan, a percussion ensemble got the message and stood with their
hands folded and their heads slightly bowed. A traffic helicopter
whacked by overhead. Taxi drivers leaned on their horns.

At the Maverick Hall in Woodstock, the recitalist Pedja Muzijevic stepped to the stage and took David Tudor's former seat at the
piano. Muzijevic, whose path has led him from Sarajevo to the
touring pianist's universe, introduced *4'33"*: "The reason we do

anything from the past is because it has application to the present. The whole interest of 'nothing coming at you' is so different now than it was in 1952." We are bombarded now, he said. He sat, unmoving, without lifting his hands or changing position. Everyone simply sat silently with him, gratefully.

> Cage: [E]veryday life is more interesting than forms of celebration, when we become aware of it. That *when* is when our intentions go down to zero. Then suddenly you notice that the world is magical.

We observe that *4'33"* is always itself, and it's always wide open to everything. This apparent paradox is actually the piece's perfection. It gives perfect freedom to performers, even though they may misunderstand and misinterpret. And it gives a perfect opening to people, who will unfailingly reveal who they are: arrogant, dismissive, argumentative and/or peaceful, accepting, reverent. The sarcastic comments on YouTube in response to the orchestral performance of *4'33"* at the Barbican in 2004 are a case in point.

Having seen the emptiness of ego noise, however, we are unruffled. Even the flaming rage of the anonymous Woodstock letter writer takes its place in a world of shadows.

INFINITY

In Suzuki's world—the world of Hua-yen Buddhism and the *Heart Sutra*—zero is a metaphor for *shunyata*, emptiness. As Suzuki said in *Third Series, shunya* equals "zero." Shunyata, then, is zero magnified to a universal principle, a statement about the absolute.

Suzuki doesn't say much about zero in *Third Series,* and he probably didn't devote much time to it in his first classes on Zen at Columbia, since he was rushing to present the complex teachings of the *Flower Garland Sutra* and the *Heart Sutra*. But at other times, according to people who attended his Columbia course, he would devote whole class sessions to zero.

And he did write about zero elsewhere. In an article he prepared for *Zen and the Birds of Appetite,* a little book by the American Catholic monk Thomas Merton, Suzuki said this:

> Metaphysically speaking, it is the mind that realizes the truth of Emptiness, and when this is done it knows that there is no self, no ego, no *Atman* [an eternal ego soul] that will pollute the mind, which is a state of zero. It is out of this zero that all good is performed and all evil is avoided. The zero I speak of is not a mathematical symbol. It is the infinite—a storehouse or womb (*Garbha*) of all possible good or values.
>
> zero = infinity, and infinity = zero.
>
> The double equation is to be understood not only statically but dynamically. It takes place between being and becoming.

A few pages later, Suzuki gently warns against the illusion that we are achieving something or going somewhere by "emptying out." What would you get rid of? Where is the trash bin? He continues:

> Zen emptiness is not the emptiness of nothingness, but the emptiness of fullness in which there is "no gain, no loss, no increase, no decrease," in which this equation takes place: zero = infinity. The Godhead is no other than this equation.

And when the Godhead (emptiness) is not dualistically separated from the world (form)—when *form is emptiness* and *emptiness is form*—then it's all right here. Where else would it be? The nondual Tao is the Way, Suzuki continued, in words that recall the koan about eating the piece of cake:

> The strange thing, however, is: when we experience it, we cease to ask questions about it, we accept it, we just live it.

Theologians, dialecticians and existentialists may go on discussing the matter, but the ordinary people . . . live "the mystery." A Zen master was once asked:

Q. What is Tao? (We may take Tao as meaning the ultimate truth or reality.)
A. It is one's everyday mind.
Q. What is one's everyday mind?
A. When tired, you sleep; when hungry, you eat.

Inevitably, Cage ran into interviewers who insisted on turning shunyata, the Godhead, into an intellectual experience. He kept urging them to "eat the cake" (so to speak), but—not surprisingly—they didn't get it. Just live the mystery, he said. But they struggled through their fog and confusion.

[Q]: It would then be false to think that Zen sets an end, a stop, a goal for itself—which would, for example, be the state of illumination in which all things reveal themselves as nothingness.
[Cage]: This nothingness is still just a word.
[Q]: Like silence, it must cancel itself out.
[Cage]: And consequently we come back to what exists; to sounds, that is.
[Q]: But don't you lose something?
[Cage]: What?
[Q]: Silence, nothingness. . . .
[Cage]: You see quite well that I'm losing *nothing*! In all of this, it's not a question of *losing*, but of *gaining*!

INTO THE MUSIC

Cage has just given *4'33"* its public airing. He has finally been able to find a form for the silence he's been nurturing for decades. In that null zone, that place of quiet and surcease, that zero of transformation, there is a pivot.

Cage has reached the peak of the mountain. Up here the view is glorious and inhospitable. His hair is tumbled and frosted by a stiff wind. He balances precariously on the rocky summit. He is a human projectile in the domain of blue. Below him lies the ordinary world's woven carpet of trees, roads, kitchens, beds. All around him, up here, an elèment bubbles through his bloodstream yet alienates his body. Where he stands, sky is everywhere; there is nowhere that isn't touched by it. The view is vast and empty.

He can't grasp it. And he can't live here. Now what? A Zen teacher will tell you: The next step always leads back down, into the music.

[Q:] The basic message of *Silence* seems to be that everything is permitted.

[Cage:] Everything is permitted if zero is taken as the basis. That's the part that isn't often understood. If you're nonintentional, then everything is permitted. If you're intentional, for instance if you want to murder someone, then it's not permitted. The same thing can be true musically.

NOT ENOUGH OF NOTHING

It's 1954, two years after the debut of *4'33"*. Cage and Tudor are scheduled to perform at the Donaueschingen music festival in Germany that September. In October, Cage will go on to speak at the Composers' Concourse in London. He expects to have time to prepare the London talk while he and Tudor sail to Europe. But the ship collides with another vessel and returns to port, and Cage and Tudor are forced to fly to Amsterdam. Cage loses his anticipated free time to write.

As he relates in his book *Silence,* he feverishly pieced together the speech in trains and hotel lobbies and restaurants during his European tour. The London talk, "45' for a Speaker," uses chance operations to wedge together fragments of earlier texts and new realizations. Huang Po's instructions to let go of thoughts interpenetrate with comments on chance and the *I Ching,* and occasional phrases from Cage's "Lecture on Nothing" and his "Lecture on Something."

This talk is something of a chopped salad, so it's intriguing that Suzuki's teachings on zero are flavoring Cage's thinking. In "45' for a Speaker," Cage has noticed the emptiness of the categories and rules advocated by Schoenberg and the proponents of twelve-tone music:

> However there is a story I have found very helpful. What's so interesting about technique anyway? *What if there are twelve tones in a row?* What row? This seeing of cause and effect is not emphasized but instead one makes an identification with what is here and now. He then spoke of two qualities. Unimpededness and Interpenetration.

"*What if there are twelve tones in a row?* What row?" Could Cage have written that observation without Suzuki's lectures on the *Heart Sutra*?

Cage adds instructions to the talk—"Bang fist on table"—"Yawn"—"Lean on elbow"—that must have turned the piece into performance art. These nonsensical actions are scattered among phrases from his great turning moments, such as the one in the anechoic chamber:

> Form
> is what interests everyone and fortunately
> it is wherever you are and there is
> no place where it isn't. Highest truth,
> that is.

If You're Lucky, Your Heart Will Break

James Ishmael Ford

*For all Buddhism's philosophy and systems, enlightenment is at heart
something mysterious, beyond our logic, plans, or will. All we can do is lay
the groundwork with our discipline, good intentions, and openness, and see
what happens. As Zen teacher and Unitarian minister James Ishmael Ford
tells us, we don't know when, how, or why awakening will happen—when
our heart will break open. But it will.*

Many years ago I was living in a Zen Buddhist monastery in Oakland, California. We sat in formal Zen meditation for several hours
every day, except during the monthly retreats when we sat for ten or
eleven hours each day—and if you've never tried it, I should say that
is physically challenging. In fact it involves a certain consistent level
of pain. However, I don't recall much of the sitting, nor of the pain.
Nor do I recall the liturgical life in any detail, nor the formal study,
nor even the regular round of work. What I do recall, vividly, is how
I was always hungry.

One evening I was eating a thin vegetable soup, feeling seriously
sorry for myself. How in the world had I gotten myself into such a
mess? Perhaps late that night I would simply pack my belongings—

didn't have too many of those to worry about—and slip away. Or, at least I could go to the nearest taqueria. And I knew of one just a few blocks away. A nice big beef burrito would certainly hit the spot.

Of course the practice was paying attention. Attending while sitting in meditation, yes, but also attending while working, while reading, while doing everything, including, of course, and very much so, eating. So reluctantly I drew myself back from that little reverie involving refried beans, sautéed vegetables, pulled spiced beef, *pico de gallo*, and maybe just a hint of guacamole, and returned to my thin, thin soup.

I'd quickly eaten all the vegetables and all that was left was—have I mentioned?—a very thin broth, but with a miso base, so cloudy I couldn't see to the bottom of the bowl. I stirred absently, watching small whirls of clouds appear and disappear in the soup. Another wave of regret and sorrow washed over me. But again I returned to the moment, to attending to the meal, such as it was, in front of me. As I just looked, a cabbage leaf floated up to the surface. I was ecstatic, absolutely ecstatic.

Then something magical happened. As I just watched, I had this amazing sense of gratitude for that cabbage leaf. And I felt gratitude for my companions in this strange project to which I'd committed myself. Then I was aware of our neighbors in the city and of the city itself. I felt gratitude for them and the people of the state and the country and the globe.

I felt a sense of joy wash through the cosmos itself. And then there I was, just me looking at that cabbage leaf. There was only that cabbage leaf floating there in front of me. No stories about it, no stories about me. Just this. Nothing more. I slipped the cabbage leaf onto my spoon, raised it to my mouth, and ate it.

The gratitude was a setup. The payoff was just slipping the cabbage leaf onto the spoon, just that motion, then raising it to my mouth, just that raising, just that moment. And just eating. Just this. Just this. The words, oh God, the words fail. But the consequences have played out for a lifetime.

It was just a taste. But it was, for me, the taste of awakening.

Awakening happens.

You don't earn it. You don't have to be good. You don't have to be smart. Awakening just happens.

And it comes to us in surprising places and times, sometimes while meditating or on retreat, or slurping down a cabbage leaf, but actually a bit more likely while washing dishes, or chasing an errant three-year-old, or sitting on the toilet.

Awakening comes to us in the most unexpected ways, in the most unexpected times. It is a gift. It is always a gift. And it comes to us like being hit by a bus.

There are many, many practices out there that claim to help. And here's a little secret: too many of them do nothing. The Unitarian Universalist theologian James Luther Adams once wryly noted how "Nothing sells like egoism wrapped in idealism." Much of what passes for spiritual practice is just puffing up the ego, reinforcing and guarding it against any and all assault. And—have no doubt in this matter—a real spiritual practice plays rough with the ego.

And the Zen path is, in this regard and others, a real spiritual practice. And it is worth pursuing, wholeheartedly. But keep your wits about you; be reasonable. Don't exaggerate any one experience. And, equally important, don't diminish it, either. Engage it all with a spirit of invitation, and maybe you'll begin to notice gratitude welling up from somewhere deep within. Whatever, somehow, your insight will appear, your awakening, your gate into the wide world and your initiation into knowing you truly are part of the great Empty family.

Have a little courage and maintain some diligence. Diligence is important.

Once I was in a meeting of Zen teachers and we were discussing what defines a real practice. One of the teachers wanted to express the finest and the highest, to outline a way that encompassed the whole of a life. It was rather beautiful. And I was more than passingly annoyed. I'm more petty, small-minded. I want to know what the minimums are. Sadly, what I've come to see is that there is no one who can tell a person what exactly must be done in order to harvest the possibilities of Zen practice. There are just too many variables to make any one-size-fits-all assertion.

Here's a hard fact. Just sitting once a week is not a Zen practice. It's true that you might wake up with that one sit. But I wouldn't put a lot of money on that likelihood. I think for most of us sitting a minimum of about a half an hour a day, most days of the week, is the baseline. And if you can also throw in some retreats—half-day, full-day, multi-day—once in a while, that's generally even better. The majority of serious Zen practitioners do more than this. But I also need to hold this up: some who have truly found the Zen way in their own hearts do less.

But be careful. Doing less than this, particularly at the beginning, when trying to find your way into Zen, sets up the distinct possibility of a dilettante practice, growing something with no roots and little chance of fruition. And, again, no one knows precisely what makes a real Zen practice, at least in terms of how much is enough. So, bottom line: just do your best. And when you find you're not, which is what most of us have experienced, often over and over, just pick yourself up, dust yourself off, and start again.

The way is vast and endlessly forgiving.

It is also harsh, demanding everything from us. But this "everything" is not about how much time you choose to put on the pillow.

Now, the truth is that even getting to that half hour a day can be difficult. While this is changing, there are still relatively few places in the country where one can find a center that offers a place to sit on a daily basis. I have little doubt that would be the best way to do it. I was blessed with living in an area with multiple centers where I could sit on just about any day of the week. And there's an amazing power in sitting with others. But looking around North America, there aren't that many such centers. Most likely, if one finds a center, it is going to offer a sitting opportunity once a week. So use it. And cultivate your own practice.

At the beginning, I recommend that regularity is vastly more important than duration. So, if you determine to sit three days a week for ten minutes a shot, and you do it, you're on your way. I've met too many people who, caught in the passion of the moment, declare they will sit two hours a day for the rest of their lives. They don't. And often, embarrassed, they disappear.

Stretch a little beyond what seems comfortable. Sit at least a little most every day. And plod on. Forgive yourself your failures, but resume. Fall down, pick yourself up, dust yourself off, and start over again. One teacher liked to say, "Fall down nine times, get up ten." Start over.

That's the practice.

Impermanence Is
Buddha Nature

Zoketsu Norman Fischer

This fine teaching by Zen teacher Zoketsu Norman Fischer is proof of the ripening and deepening of Buddhism in America. In it he connects the teachings of one of Buddhism's most difficult philosophers, Dogen, with the fundamental truths taught by the Buddha and moving personal stories of his own life. Change isn't just a reality we have to accept and work with, says Fischer. It is enlightenment itself, manifesting moment by moment in time.

The scene of the Buddha's passing, as told in the Pali canon's *Mahaparinibbana Sutta*, is starkly beautiful. The Buddha, having previously "renounced the life force" and announced the time and place of his passing, is surrounded by his disciples. He asks them if they have any last questions or doubts, and through their silence (and his clairvoyance), he realizes that they are all well established in awakening. He then pronounces his final words to them and to all subsequent generations of practitioners: "Now monks, I declare to you: all conditioned things have the nature of vanishing. Keep on diligently with your practice!" Then the Buddha journeys back and forth through the various meditation states, finally passing from this life. Those monks not yet fully awakened "tore their hair, raised their arms, threw themselves down twisting and turning, and cried out in their extreme grief, 'Too soon! Too soon!'" But the fully awakened monastics remained mindful, saying, "All compound things are impermanent. What's the use of crying?"

Practitioners have always understood impermanence as the cornerstone of Buddhist teachings and practice. All that exists is impermanent; nothing lasts. Therefore nothing can be grasped or held on to. When we don't fully appreciate this simple but profound truth we suffer, as did the monks who descended into misery and despair at the Buddha's passing. When we do, we have real peace and understanding, as did the monks who remained fully mindful and calm.

As far as classical Buddhism is concerned, impermanence is the number one inescapable, and essentially painful, fact of life. It is the singular existential problem that the whole edifice of Buddhist practice is meant to address. To understand impermanence at the deepest possible level (we all understand it at superficial levels), and to merge with it fully, is the whole of the Buddhist path. The Buddha's final words express this: Impermanence is inescapable. Everything vanishes. Therefore, there is nothing more important than continuing the path with diligence. All other options either deny or shortshrift the problem.

A while ago I had a dream that has stayed with me. In a hazy grotto, my mother-in-law and I, coming from opposite directions, are trying to squeeze through a dim doorway. Both of us are fairly large people and the space is small, so for a moment we are stuck together in the doorway. Finally we press through, she to her side (formerly mine), I to mine (formerly hers).

It's not that surprising to me that I would dream about my mother-in-law. Her situation is often on my mind. My mother-in-law is nearing ninety. She has many health problems. She is usually in pain, can't walk and sleep at night, and is losing the use of her hands to neuropathy. She lives with her husband of more than sixty years, who has advanced Alzheimer's disease, can't speak a coherent sentence, and doesn't know who or where he is. Despite all this, my mother-in-law affirms life 100 percent, as she always has. She never entertains the idea of death, as far as I know. All she wants and hopes for is a good and pleasant life. Since she doesn't have this right now (though she hasn't given up hope for it), she is fairly miserable, as anyone in her situation would be.

I, on the other hand, am fairly healthy, with no expectation of dying anytime soon. Yet from childhood I have been thinking about death, and the fact of death has probably been the main motivator in my life. (Why else would I have devoted myself full-time to Buddhist practice from an early age?) Consequently, almost all my talking and writing, and much of my thinking, is in one way or another in reference to death, absence, disappearing.

So this dream intrigues and confuses me. Is my mother-in-law about to pass over from life to death, though temporarily stuck in the crowded doorway? If that's the logic of the dream, then I must be dead, stuck in that same doorway as I try to pass through to life. Of course, this makes no sense! But then, the longer I contemplate life and death, the less sense they make. Sometimes I wonder whether life and death isn't merely a conceptual framework we confuse ourselves with. Of course, people do seem to disappear, and, this having been the case generally with others, it seems reasonable to assume that it will be the case for us at some point. But how to understand this? And how to account for the many anomalies that appear when you look closely, such as reported appearances of ghosts and other visitations from the dead, reincarnation, and so on?

It is very telling that some religions refer to death as "eternal life," and that in the *Mahaparinibbana Sutta* the Buddha doesn't die. He enters *parinirvana*, full extinction, which is something other than death. In Buddhism generally, death isn't death—it's a staging area for further life. So there are many respectable and less respectable reasons to wonder about the question of death.

There are a lot of older people in the Buddhist communities in which I practice. Some are in their seventies and eighties, and others in their sixties, like me. Because of this, the theme of death and impermanence is always on our minds and seems to come up again and again in the teachings we study. All conditioned things pass away. Nothing remains as it was. The body changes and weakens as it ages. In response to this, and to a lifetime's experience, the mind changes as well. The way one thinks of, views, and feels about life and the world is different. Even the same thoughts one had in youth or midlife take on a different flavor when held in older age. The other day a friend about my age, who in her youth studied Zen with the great master Song Sa Nim, told me, "He always said, 'Soon dead!' I understood the words then as being true: very Zen, and almost funny. Now they seem personal and poignant."

"All conditioned things have the nature of vanishing." What is impermanence after all? When we're young we know that death is coming, but it will probably come later, so we don't have to be so concerned with it now. And even if we are concerned with it in youth, as I was, the concern is philosophical. When we are older we know death is coming sooner rather than later, so we take it more personally. But do we really know what we are talking about?

Death may be the ultimate loss, the ultimate impermanence, but even on a lesser, everyday scale, impermanence and the loss it entails still happens more or less "later." Something is here now in a particular way; later it will not be. I am or have something now; later I will not. But "later" is the safest of all time frames. It can be safely ignored because it's not now—it's later, and later never comes. And even if it does, we don't have to worry about it now. We can worry about it later. For most of us most of the time, impermanence seems irrelevant.

But in truth, impermanence isn't later; it's now. "All conditioned things have the nature of vanishing." Right now, as they appear before us, they have that nature. It's not that something vanishes later. Right now, everything is in some way—though we don't understand in what way—vanishing before our very eyes. Squeezing uncomfortably through the narrow doorway of now, we don't know whether we are coming or going. Impermanence may be a deeper thought than we at first appreciate.

Impermanence is not only loss; it is also change, and change can be refreshing, renewing. In fact, change is always both good and bad, because change, even when it is refreshing, always entails loss. Nothing new appears unless something old ceases. As they say on New Year's Eve, "Out with the old, in with the new," a happy and a sad occasion. As with the scene in the *Mahaparinibbana Sutta*, there's despair and equanimity at the same time. Impermanence is both.

In one of his most important essays, the great twelfth-century Japanese Zen master Dogen writes, "Impermanence is itself Buddha Nature." This seems quite different from the classical Buddhist notion of impermanence, which emphasizes the loss side of the loss-change-renewal equation. For Dogen, impermanence isn't a problem to be overcome with diligent effort on the path. Impermanence *is* the path. Practice isn't the way to cope with or overcome impermanence. It is the way to fully appreciate and live it.

"If you want to understand Buddha Nature," Dogen writes, "you should intimately observe cause and effect over time. When the time is ripe, Buddha Nature manifests." In explaining this teaching, Dogen, in his usual inside-out, upside-down way (Dogen is unique among Zen masters in his intricately detailed literary style, which usually involves very counterconceptual ways of understanding typical concepts), writes that practice isn't so much a matter of changing or improving the conditions of your inner or outer life, as a way of fully embracing and appreciating those conditions, especially the condition of impermanence and loss. When you practice, "the time becomes ripe." While this phrase naturally implies a "later" (something unripe ripens in time), Dogen understands it is the opposite way: Time is always ripe. Buddha Nature always manifests in time, because time is always impermanence.

Of course, time is impermanence and impermanence is time! Time is change, development, loss. Present time is ungraspable: as soon as it occurs, it immediately falls into the past. As soon as I am here, I am gone. If this were not so, how could the me of this moment ever give way to the me of the following moment? Unless the first me disappears, clearing the way, the second me cannot appear.

So my being here is thanks to my not being here. If I were not not here, I couldn't be here!

In words, this becomes very quickly paradoxical and absurd, but in living, it seems to be exactly the case. Logically it must be so, and once in a while (especially in a long meditation retreat) you can actually, viscerally, feel it. Nothing appears unless it appears in time. And whatever appears in time appears and vanishes at once, just as the Buddha said on his deathbed. Time is existence, impermanence, change, loss, growth, development—the best and the worst news at once. Dogen calls this strange immense process Buddha Nature. "Buddha Nature is no other than *all are*, because *all are* is Buddha Nature," he writes. The phrase *all are* is telling. *Are*: existence, being, time, impermanence, change. *All are*: existence, being, time, impermanence, change is never lonely; it is always all-inclusive. We're all always in this together.

The other day I was talking to an old friend, an experienced Zen practitioner, about her practice. She told me she was beginning to notice that the persistent feeling of dissatisfaction she always felt in relation to others, to the world, and to the circumstances of her inner and outer life, was probably not about others, the world, or inner and outer circumstances, but instead was about her deepest inmost self itself. Dissatisfaction, she said, seems in some way to *be* herself, to be fundamentally engrained in her. Before realizing this, she went on, she'd assumed her dissatisfaction was due in some way to a personal failing on her part—a failing that she had hoped to correct with her Zen practice. But now she could see that it was far worse than that! The dissatisfaction was not *about* her, and therefore correctable; it was built *into* her, it was essential to her self!

This seems to be exactly what the Buddha meant when he spoke of the basic shakiness of our sense of subjectivity in the famous doctrine of *anatta*, or non-self. Though we all need healthy egos to operate normally in the world, the essential grounding of ego is the false notion of permanence, a notion that we unthinkingly subscribe to, even though, deep in our hearts, we know it's untrue. I am me, I have been me, I will be me. I can change, and I want to change, but

I am always here, always me, and have never known any other experience. But this ignores the reality that "all conditioned things have the nature of vanishing," and are vanishing constantly, as a condition of their existing in time, whose nature is vanishing.

No wonder we feel, as my friend felt, a constant nagging sense of dissatisfaction and disjunction that we might well interpret as coming from a chronic personal failing (that is, once we'd gotten over the even more faulty belief that others were responsible for it). On the other hand, "*all are* is Buddha Nature." This means that the self is not, as we imagine, an improvable, permanent, isolated entity we and we alone are responsible for; instead it is impermanence itself, which is never alone, never isolated, constantly flowing, and immense: Buddha Nature itself.

Dogen writes "Impermanence itself is Buddha Nature." And adds, "Permanence is the mind that discriminates the wholesomeness and unwholesomeness of all things." Permanence!? Impermanence seems to be (as Dogen himself writes elsewhere) an "unshakable teaching" in buddhadharma. How does "permanence" manage to worm its way into Dogen's discourse?

I come back to my dream of being stuck in the doorway between life and death with my mother-in-law: which side is which, and who is going where? Impermanence and permanence may simply be balancing concepts—words, feelings, and thoughts that support one another in helping us grope toward an understanding (and a misunderstanding) of our lives. For Dogen, "permanence" is practice: having the wisdom and the commitment to see the difference between what we commit ourselves to pursuing in this human lifetime, and what we commit ourselves to letting go of. The good news in "impermanence is Buddha Nature" is that we can finally let ourselves off the hook: we can let go of the great and endless chore of improving ourselves, of being stellar accomplished people, inwardly or in our external lives. This is no small thing, because we are all subject to this kind of brutal inner pressure to be and do more today than we have been and done yesterday—and more than someone else has been and done today and tomorrow.

On the other hand, the bad news in "impermanence is Buddha Nature" is that it's so big there isn't much we can do with it. It can't be enough simply to repeat the phrase to ourselves. And if we are not striving to accomplish the Great Awakening, the Ultimate Improvement, what would we do, and why would we do it? Dogen asserts a way and a motivation. If impermanence is the worm at the heart of the apple of self, making suffering a built-in factor of human life, then permanence is the petal emerging from the sepal of the flower of impermanence. It makes happiness possible. Impermanence *is* permanent, the ongoing process of living and dying and time. Permanence is nirvana, bliss, cessation, relief—the never-ending, ever-changing, and growing field of practice.

In the Buddha's final scene as told in the sutra, the contrast between the monastics who tore their hair, raised their arms, and threw themselves down in their grief and those who received the Buddha's passing with equanimity couldn't be greater. The sutra seems to imply disapproval of the former and approval of the latter. Or perhaps the approval and disapproval are in our reading. For if impermanence is permanence is Buddha Nature, then loss is loss is also happiness, and both sets of monastics are to be approved. Impermanence is not only to be overcome and conquered. It is also to be lived and appreciated, because it reflects the *all are* side of our human nature. The weeping and wailing monastics were not only expressing their attachment; they were also expressing their immersion in this human life, and their love for someone they revered.

I have experienced this more than once at times of great loss. While I may not tear my hair and throw myself down in my grieving, I have experienced extreme sadness and loss, feeling the whole world weeping and dark with the fresh absence of someone I love. At the same time I have felt some appreciation and equanimity, because loss, searing as it can be, is also beautiful, sad and beautiful. My tears, my sadness, are beautiful because they are the consequence of love, and my grieving makes me love the world and life all the more. Every loss I have ever experienced, every personal and emotional teaching of impermanence that life has been kind enough to offer me, has deepened my ability to love.

The happiness that spiritual practice promises is not endless bliss, endless joy, and soaring transcendence. Who would want that in a world in which there is so much injustice, so much tragedy, so much unhappiness, illness, and death? To feel the scourge of impermanence and loss and to appreciate it at the same time profoundly as the beautiful essence of what it means to be at all—this is the deep truth I hear reverberating in the Buddha's last words. Everything vanishes. Practice goes on.

Living Fully

Shyalpa Tenzin Rinpoche

Working with our thoughts is the greatest challenge in meditation—as it is in life. The Vajrayana master Shyalpa Tenzin Rinpoche shows us how to transform our thoughts into the wisdom they truly are, so that we can experience them not as imprisonment but as freedom.

Destructive habits and careless behavior are the cause of our suffering. If we seek to live our lives fully, we should not become trapped in our routines. When a bee settles on a flower to suck its nectar, it is intoxicated by the taste. Unaware that night is descending, the bee is trapped in the flower as the petals slowly close. As human beings, we should use our intelligence and hone our awareness so that our habits do not shackle us and rob us of our freedom.

Discursive thoughts and afflictive emotions obscure the naturally expansive and luminous nature of mind. Awareness is lost when we narrowly focus on ourselves and what the "I" experiences. This tunnel vision creates the breeding ground for a strong sense of ego. When we cannot transcend our ordinary, habitual ways of thinking, we become mired in our confusion. Not recognizing the pristine nature of mind, we suffer because there is a great deal of attachment to the "I." An endless stream of thoughts, with one thought linked to the next, traps us in a perpetual cycle of confusion and pain.

Each thought should remain in its own place. It would not make sense to drag a caterpillar from its cocoon and expect it to make honey; that would be unnatural. Similarly, if you placed a honeybee in a cocoon, it would not know how to transform into a butterfly. So the caterpillar should remain in its cocoon, and the honeybee should make honey. When you experience each thought in its completeness, the energy of the thought arises and dissolves in its own place. Therefore, you do not need to tamper with your thoughts. Further elaboration causes bewilderment and confusion. When the energy of each thought is complete and independent, it is liberated upon arising and leaves no trace.

If you cannot see the nature of each thought as complete and independent, it is because you are attached to the "I" and what the "I" creates. When you think, "I am going to do this," you create continuity for the "I." If you think, "I want this," you mentally select one button, and if you think, "I want that," you select the next button. There is no space for each thought to be complete and independent because you are thriving on the illusion of continuity. One could say that an independent thought is natural energy that is fresh, vivid awareness. It is not dependent upon further support.

When you follow your thoughts in pursuit of an illusory "I," your entanglement with each thought enslaves you. This mental confusion compels you to follow the first thought with a second thought, the second thought with a third thought, and so on, and so on. Therefore, each thought does not exist independently. We write our own story based on an illusory self. Bound in an endless chain of confused thoughts, we suffer in a vicious cycle of misery, which we call samsara. Samsara is the state of unenlightened ignorance. Unaware of the pure nature of mind and experience, one is helplessly controlled by disturbing emotions and karma, and one experiences an endless stream of mental and physical stress and suffering.

During the practice of meditation, we experience gaps in the flow of thoughts, and this space allows us to relax and loosen the grip of entrenched habits and reactive behavior. Glimpses of space in our mental landscape slowly free us from a tangled web of discursive thoughts and allow us to live more fully in the luminous present. Meditation is an effective tool for breaking free of deep-seated habits. Other methods, such as those offered in some self-help books, attempt to replace negative habits with positive thinking, but this does not address the real source of the problem. If we wish to free ourselves from our habits, the most effective approach is to ask ourselves, "Who is bound by habit, and how do these habits originate?"

The frequently quoted metaphor of the lion and the dog illustrates this approach. If you throw a stone at a dog, the dog will chase after the stone. If you throw a stone at a lion, the lion will chase after you! The dog will continue to chase stones, but the lion will be finished with it once and for all. Look directly at the source of each thought rather than following its trail. Habits are conditional and fabricated by thoughts. These patterns of thought and action are the result of our failure to discover their source. Habits are a form of energy, and energy emerges and subsides like waves on the surface of the ocean. When you recognize the source, the energy will self-liberate upon arising; it will not result in more habitual behavior.

Your practice is to find the source of the stone. You can continue to behave like a restless dog chasing after each thought, or you can pounce like a fearless lion and discover that the source of your thoughts is pure energy arising from emptiness. In this state of timeless purity, nothing truly comes into existence and nothing solidly exists, so there is no obstruction. If you have the courage to rest in this vast space, the fictions that fuel your enslaving habits will find no fertile ground in which to grow.

We should not reject our thoughts and feelings, since they are all valid. However, our thoughts and feelings cause us problems when we cling to them as if they were fixed and unchanging. When we abide in the empty and spacious nature of self and phenomena, we are free from all confusion. Therefore, let everything arise as sheer inspiration. Let everything be a celebration. Whatever arises is perfectly fine, but if nothing arises, that is fine, too. With a flexible mind, we can direct our lives with sophistication. We will be beyond corruption, and no matter what happens, we will be above the fray, so to speak. When we recognize the luminous quality of our true nature, clear essence will appear everywhere. This is amazing indeed!

Not for Happiness

Dzongsar Jamyang Khyentse

Dzongsar Jamyang Khyentse is one of the truth-tellers of contemporary Buddhism. He informs us that if the goal of our Buddhist practice is happiness, it may not be the real thing. But if you're looking for painful truths, searching self-examination, and freedom from self-cherishing, then Buddhism is the religion for you.

Buddhist practices are techniques we use to tackle our habitual self-cherishing. Each one is designed to attack individual habits until the compulsion to cling to "self" is entirely eradicated. So, although a practice may look Buddhist, if it reinforces self-clinging, it is actually far more dangerous than any overtly non-Buddhist practice.

The aim of far too many teachings these days is to make people "feel good," and even some Buddhist masters are beginning to sound like New Age apostles. Their talks are entirely devoted to validating the manifestation of ego and endorsing the "rightness" of our feelings, neither of which have anything to do with the teachings we find in the pith instructions. So, if you are only concerned about feeling good, you are far better off having a full-body massage or listening to some uplifting or life-affirming music than receiving dharma teachings, which were definitely not designed to cheer you up. On the contrary, the dharma was devised specifically to expose your failings and make you feel awful.

Try reading *The Words of My Perfect Teacher*. If you find it depressing, if Patrul Rinpoche's disconcerting truths rattle your worldly self-confidence, be happy. It is a sign that at long last you are beginning to understand something about the dharma. And by the way, to feel depressed is not always a bad thing. It is completely understandable for someone to feel depressed and deflated when their most humiliating failing is exposed. Who wouldn't feel a bit raw in such a situation? But isn't it better to be painfully aware of a failing rather than utterly oblivious to it? If a flaw in your character remains hidden, how can you do anything about it? So, although pith instructions might temporarily depress you, they will also help uproot your shortcomings by dragging them into the open. This is what is meant by the phrase "dharma penetrating your mind," or, as the great Jamgön Kongtrul Lodrö Tayé put it, "the practice of dharma bearing fruit," rather than the so-called good experiences too many of us hope for, such as good dreams, blissful sensations, ecstasy, clairvoyance, or the enhancement of intuition.

Patrul Rinpoche said there is no such thing as a person who has perfected both dharma practice and worldly life, and if we ever meet someone who appears to be good at both, the likelihood is that his skills are grounded in worldly values.

It is such a mistake to assume that practicing dharma will help us calm down and lead an untroubled life; nothing could be further from the truth. Dharma is not a therapy. Quite the opposite, in fact; dharma is tailored specifically to turn your life upside down—it's what you sign up for. So when your life goes pear-shaped, why do you complain? If you practice and your life fails to capsize, it is a sign that what you are doing is not working. This is what distinguishes the dharma from New Age methods involving auras, relationships, communication, well-being, the Inner Child, being one with the universe, and tree hugging. From the point of view of dharma, such interests are the toys of samsaric beings—toys that quickly bore us senseless.

The "Heart of Sadness"

Kongtrul Rinpoche suggested we pray to the guru, buddhas, and bodhisattvas and ask them to grant their blessings, "So I may give birth to the heart of sadness." But what is a "heart of sadness"? Imagine one night you have a dream. Although it is a good dream, deep down you know that eventually you will have to wake up and it will be over. In life, too, sooner or later, whatever the state of our relationships, or our health, our jobs, and every aspect of our lives, everything, absolutely everything, will change. And the little bell ringing in the back of your head to remind you of this inevitability is what is called the "heart of sadness." Life, you realize, is a race against time, and you should never put off dharma practice until next year, next month, or tomorrow, because the future may never happen.

This race-against-time kind of attitude is so important, especially when it comes to practice. My own experience has shown me that promising myself I will start to practice next week more or less guarantees that I never get around to it. And I don't think I am alone. So, once you understand that real dharma practice is not just about formal sitting meditation, but a never-ending confrontation with and opposition to pride and ego, as well as a lesson in how to accept change, you will be able to start practicing right away. For example, imagine you are sitting on a beach admiring the sunset. Nothing terrible has happened and you are content, even happy. Then suddenly that little bell starts to ring in your head, reminding you that this could be the last sunset you ever see. You realize that, were you to die, you might not be reborn with the ability to appreciate a sunset, let alone the capacity to understand what a sunset is, and this thought alone helps you focus your mind on practice.

Go beyond Concept

A sincere wish to practice the dharma is not born of a desire for personal happiness or to be perceived as a "good" person, but neither do we practice because we want to be unhappy or become "bad" people. A genuine aspiration to practice dharma arises from the longing to attain enlightenment.

By and large, human beings tend to prefer to fit in to society by following accepted rules of etiquette and being gentle, polite, and respectful. The irony is that this is also how most people imagine a spiritual person should behave. When a so-called dharma practitioner is seen to behave badly, we shake our heads over her audacity at presenting herself as a follower of the Buddha. Yet such judgments are better avoided, because to "fit in" is not what a genuine dharma practitioner strives for. Think of the great mahasiddha Tilopa, for example. He looked so outlandish that if he turned up on your doorstep today, odds are you would refuse to let him in. And you would have a point. He would most probably be almost completely naked (if you were lucky, he might be sporting some kind of G-string); his hair would never have been introduced to shampoo; and protruding from his mouth would quiver the tail of a live fish. What would your moral judgment be of such a being? "Him! A Buddhist? But he's tormenting that poor creature by eating it alive!" This is how our theistic, moralistic, and judgmental minds work. In fact, they work in a very similar way to those of the world's more puritanical and destructive religions. Of course, there is nothing necessarily wrong with morality, but the point of spiritual practice, according to the Vajrayana teachings, is to go beyond all our concepts, including those of morality.

Right now the majority of us can only afford to be slightly non-conformist, yet we should aspire to be like Tilopa. We should pray that one day we will have the courage to be just as crazy by daring to go beyond the eight worldly dharmas and care not one jot about whether or not we are praised or criticized. In today's world such an attitude is the ultimate craziness. More than ever, people expect to be happy when they are admired and praised, and unhappy when derided and criticized, and so it is unlikely that those who want the world to perceive them as sane will risk flying from the nest of the eight worldly dharmas. Sublime beings, though, couldn't care less either way, and that is why, from our mundane point of view, they are considered crazy.

Develop "Renunciation Mind"

If worldly happiness is not the goal of dharma, then what is it that prompts a person to want to practice? Chances are that stepping onto a spiritual path would not even occur to a person who is rich, enjoys their life, and has a strong sense of personal security. Of course, all of us, even the rich, experience moments of sadness and hopelessness, and may even momentarily feel the urge to turn our backs on all this world has to offer. But this is not a genuine experience of renunciation mind, as it has far more to do with weariness and boredom than renunciation, and is often a sign that, like a spoilt child tired of his toys, we are in desperate need of a change.

Jamgön Kongtrul Lodrö Tayé said that if deep down you continue to believe a tiny corner of samsara could be useful or that it might even offer the ultimate solution to all your worldly problems, it will be extremely difficult to become a genuine spiritual seeker. To believe that life's problems will somehow work themselves out, everything bad is fixable, and something about samsara has to be worth fighting for makes it virtually impossible to nurture a genuine, all-consuming desire to practice the dharma. The only view that truly works for a dharma practitioner is that there are no solutions to the sufferings of samsara and it cannot be fixed.

It is vital to understand that however positive this worldly life, or even a small part of it, may appear to be, ultimately it will fail because absolutely nothing genuinely works in samsara. It is a very difficult attitude to adopt, but if we can at least accept it on an intellectual level, it will provide us with just the incentive we need to step onto the spiritual path. (Other incentives include making fools of ourselves or becoming entangled in worldly systems by trying to fix them.) The bottom line, though, is that only once a beginner truly appreciates just how hopeless and purposeless samsara really is will a genuine aspiration to follow a spiritual path arise in his mind.

As Shakyamuni Buddha, compassionately and with great courage, explained to an autocratic king, there are four inescapable realities that eventually destroy all sentient beings:

1. We will all become old and frail.
2. It is absolutely certain that everything will constantly change.
3. Everything we achieve or accumulate will eventually fall apart and scatter.
4. We are all bound to die.

Yet our emotions and habits are so strong that even when the truth is staring us in the face, we are unable to see it.

In addition to recognizing the futility of samsara, the point of dharma practice is that it penetrates our minds and diminishes our affection for our ego and worldly life by pressing us to detach ourselves from the eight worldly dharmas. However beneficial a practice appears to be, however politically correct or exciting, if it does not contradict your habit of grasping at permanence, or looks harmless but insidiously encourages you to forget the truth of impermanence and the illusory nature of phenomena, it will inevitably take you in the opposite direction to dharma.

Develop the Willingness to Face the Truth

Most of us tend to resent being confronted with the truth, and from resentment springs denial. The most obvious example is that we feel annoyed when we are forced to acknowledge the illusory nature of our lives and the reality of death. We also take exception to contemplating it, even though death is an irrefutable universal truth. Our habitual reaction is to pretend it will never happen—which is how we deal with most of the other inconvenient truths we find difficult to stomach.

Instead of becoming resentful, though, it is important for anyone who sincerely wishes to become a dharma practitioner to develop a willingness and openness to embrace the truth, because the dharma is the truth. The Buddha himself made no bones about it. He never once provided his students with rose-tinted glasses to take the edge off the horror of the truth of impermanence, the agonies that are "emotion," the illusory nature of our world, and, above all, the vast and profound truth of *shunyata*. None of these truths is easy to understand, or even to aspire to understand, particularly for minds programmed by habit to long for emotional satisfaction and aim for ordinary bliss. And so, if someone is able to hear teachings about emptiness and tolerate them intellectually as well as practically and emotionally, it is an indication that they have a real affinity for the dharma.

Overcome Poverty Mentality

Many of us feel spiritually impoverished. Kongtrul Rinpoche said this is because we never stop desiring comfort and happiness. Until that kind of poverty mentality is overcome, a large portion of our mind will always be busy trying to secure personal comfort and happiness, making letting go of anything at all extremely difficult. Even those who present themselves as spiritual practitioners will find it impossible to make the superhuman effort necessary.

The problem here is that on a superficial, worldly level, everything spiritual, especially the buddhadharma, appears to be utterly useless and a complete waste of time. We are practical beings who like to build houses so that we can be comfortable and happy, and to put our resources into erecting a stupa with no bedroom or toilet or anything functional in it strikes us as being wasteful. But as Kongtrul Rinpoche pointed out, clinging to the merest hint of an idea that worldly values and ideals might somehow be useful makes it extremely hard for anyone to tackle something as apparently futile as spiritual practice. And to cut the ties of the habits that bind us to worldly values, especially when it comes to material wealth, is virtually impossible. "Wealth," from an authentic dharma perspective, is understood entirely differently. For a dharma practitioner, wealth is not gold, silver, or a healthy bank account; wealth is contentment—the feeling that you have enough and need nothing more.

LIBERATION FROM ILLUSION AND DELUSION

As the Buddha said in the *Vajracchedika Prajnaparamita Sutra* (the *Diamond Sutra*), "Like a star, hallucination, candle, Magical illusion, dewdrop, bubble, Dream, lightning, or a cloud—Know all compounded phenomena to be like this."

From a Buddhist point of view, each aspect and moment of our lives is an illusion. According to the Buddha, it's like seeing a black spot in the sky that you are unable to make sense of, then concentrating on it intensely until finally you are able to make out a flock of birds; or hearing a perfect echo that sounds exactly like a real person shouting back at you. Life is nothing more than a continuous stream of sensory illusions, from the obvious ones, like fame and power, to those less easy to discern, like death, nosebleeds, and headaches. Tragically, though, most human beings believe in what they see, and so the truth Buddha exposed about the illusory nature of life can be a little hard to swallow.

What happens once we know that everything we see and experience is an illusion? And what is left once those illusions have been liberated? To be liberated from illusion is to dispel all the limitations that false perception brings and entirely transform our attitude. So, "liberate" means to be released from the delusion of imagining illusions to be real. But crucially, we have to want to be liberated; we have to want to become enlightened. And it is only once we develop a genuine longing for enlightenment that, almost automatically, we start to learn how not to want to be ambitious in a worldly sense. Such a longing is not easy to generate, but without it, to step aimlessly onto the spiritual path would be utterly pointless.

Millions of people in this world are interested in some version of meditation, or yoga, or one of the many so-called spiritual activities that are now so widely marketed. A closer look at why people engage in these practices reveals an aim that has little to do with

liberation from delusion, and everything do to with their despera-
tion to escape busy, unhappy lives, and heartfelt longing for a
healthy, stress-free, happy life. All of which are romantic illusions.

So, where do we find the roots of these illusions? Mainly in our
habitual patterns and their related actions. Of course, no one of
sound mind imagines any of us would willingly live an illusion. But
we are contrary beings, and even though we are convinced we would
shun a life built on self-deception, we continue to maintain a strong
grip on the habits that are the cause of countless delusions. Small
wonder the great masters of the past have said that although everyone longs to be free from suffering, most of us simply won't let go of
it; and although no one wants to suffer, we find it almost impossible
not to be attracted to samsara.

MINDFULNESS

The problem: distraction

Most of us know that aggression is a problem, as are pride and jealousy, but the truth is that all emotions cause problems one way or
another and each has a distinctive character. "Passion," for example,
is starkly different from "aggression." Fundamentally, though, all
emotions spring from one basic source, distraction.

What is "distraction"? Clearly, it is not merely the sound of a
chainsaw firing up or blaring Bollywood music that interrupts our
meditation practice. On a more profound level, distraction is any
of the emotional responses we are sidetracked by—for example,
hope for praise and fear of blame—as well as its more subtle mani-
festations, like being spaced-out, distracted, lost in thought, or
worked up.

The solution: mindfulness

Since our fundamental problem is distraction, its fundamental
solution is to be mindful. There is an infinite number of methods for
developing mindfulness that all fall into one of two categories:

shamatha or *vipashyana*. The point of *shamatha* practice is to make mind malleable. But a pliant mind alone will not uproot samsara completely; we also need to see the truth, which is why vipashyana, or insight, practice is so crucial.

Unfortunately, though, mindfulness is difficult, mostly because we lack the enthusiasm to develop it, but also because our habit of longing for distraction is both deeply ingrained and extremely tenacious. It is therefore vital for a dharma practitioner to develop renunciation mind and to recognize the defects of samsara, both of which lie at the core of the Buddhist approach to training the mind.

The masters of the past suggest we should constantly remind ourselves about: the imminence of death; the futility of our worldly activities; and the worst news of all, that there is no end to samsara's sufferings. Just look around you and you will see that the world never ceases to churn out more and more of the same thing, and that the result is unremitting pain and unbearable suffering. It's no surprise, then, as the great masters have pointed out, that to maintain mindfulness for as long as it takes to drink a cup of tea accumulates more merit than years of practicing generosity, discipline, and asceticism.

The Vagabond Queen of Craigslist

Bonnie Friedman

Hopscotching through Brooklyn, from temporary abode to temporary abode, writer Bonnie Friedman discovers the delight in nonattachment.

I wept when my husband and I had to give up our apartment in Brooklyn so I could go off and teach at the University of North Texas. My landlady simply would not let me sublet. "I'll pay a year up front!" I pled. (So what if it risked my savings?) "I'll let you approve the subletter!" (Surely we could find somebody on whom we both agreed.) It frightened me to have no home in the city in which I'd grown up—as if I'd become a stranger to myself. But the landlady was adamant: *No, no,* and *no.* She needed direct control of who lived in her building.

All that final summer I walked around the neighborhood, morose. Goodbye, fruit market on Atlantic Avenue, where sunset-orange mango chunks and beds of ruby pomegranate seeds gleamed, raising my spirits on difficult days. Two of my literary heroes had written about this roaring, ragtag thoroughfare. Frank McCourt lived for a year right over Montero's Bar after his first marriage broke up. He'd both hated and loved the place. His apartment pulsed with music and seemed a shameful spot for a schoolteacher to live in, but the bar did have its charms: one need never be alone. And here was Montero's still, with its creaking blue neon sign, its dusky interior.

And the nature writer Edward Abbey, on the very first page of *Desert Solitaire*, talked about the docks at the end of Atlantic Avenue. The fact that two of my favorite authors had referenced a street in my neighborhood made me feel a covert affinity with them, a secret strength—if they could find success despite real limitations, so could I. Oh, I did not want to give up this place! I was a mess that August day when the movers hauled my possessions down the stairs.

"But you can sublet places on Craigslist!" said my friend Sally, during our goodbye supper. "Sample other parts of the city during winter and summer break! It'll be an adventure."

I sighed. What a Pollyanna! Didn't she understand it was change itself I most disliked?

Yet Sally was right. For the past four years I've been the vagabond queen of Craigslist.com, hopscotching Brooklyn. And the adventure has been wonderful. While I live in each apartment, I study what it has to teach. I read its books, eat the food on its shelves, and consider the perspective from its windows.

Beyond that, I've been forced to undergo a spiritual education in acquiring and letting go. It's as if I were a hermit crab inhabiting one distinctive shell after another, or a reincarnate who got to live through many life cycles while being allowed to keep her memory of each.

And something has shifted in me, thanks to this reiteration of loss and gain. I've begun to internalize that this is just the way of things: alteration, change. The tide washes in innumerable things—some marvelous, some mere hard grit—then sweeps them forth. Again. And again.

I appreciate with keener delight and observe more closely each fresh place. And when it's time to return the key, it's with a more transitory sense of regret, an almost bemused sense of the lightness of being. How often I've emptied drawers of my possessions! Why act as if my happiness is suffused in these walls, interfolded with these books, dependent on the chirp of the particular bird who nests in this tree? Of course some part of me still believes that my happiness *is* all these things, totally synonymous with each place. But another part of me—brand new, marveling, even kind—gazes on and says, *Yes, yes, of course. Get teary, if you must! But haven't you learned by now, you naïf, the gift of this experience? Ah, yes: you see it for a moment, then lose track of it again!*

I nod to myself, blowing my nose, and do my best to fix my gaze out the cab's front window, instead of at the receding image of my latest temporary residence.

My first winter break I found an apartment in Red Hook, near the Columbia waterfront—a loft owned by a graphic artist with a truly lovely eye. There was a Parisian kitchen with black-and-white floor tile and dangling copper pots, and a living room with dozens of seriously flourishing plants—a source of worry, since houseplants tend to wither under my care. I took pages of notes on when to water and learned to assess soil with my fingertips and notice the precise tinge of leaves. My first morning in that sequestered apartment I woke up and lay in bed, astonished. Opulent silence enfolded me, luscious as mink. Who knew the city could be this serene?

I'd always lived in apartments that were more centrally located and that carried the city's clang; one of them even jounced up and down like an elevator with each passing truck. I'd no idea the city also had such pockets of silence.

The Red Hook artist's space was so pretty that I was inspired to keep it neat, and that, in turn, led me to host a dinner party. I invited friends for New Year's and ordered trays of pasta and chicken from Cucina Napoletana. My friends had never been inside any apartment with my name on the lease; I'm usually so messy that no one's allowed in. Yet now I discovered the pleasure of trying to give a beautiful evening to friends.

The shelves in that first apartment held a book with photos of Stanley Kunitz's garden, accompanied by his poems. I read and reread the poems and gazed at the cobalt-blue irises and sheaves of lavender. The flowers rose out of soil that Kunitz had created himself from years of mulching seaweed.

After decades of reading only prose, the rediscovery of the concision of poetry! And after a lifetime of asphalt, the revelation that soil itself is something you can grow!

Gin stood poised on a high shelf in the kitchen of this apartment. If I couldn't sleep, I stood on a chair and fetched the Beefeater's, adding tonic water from the icy fridge. Yum! And then: blotto—a velvet sledgehammer delivered me into blank unconsciousness. I rarely drank gin. But the entire time I was in that apartment I allowed myself, if I woke up during the night, to sip. And to eat the crystallized ginger in the Mason jar. I was Goldilocks. What fun to try out everything!

The very last day I replaced what I'd taken, and a hollow sadness shook me. I looked out the rear cab window, confused by loss all over again, as the driver took me to LaGuardia. It didn't matter that I'd known from the outset my stay was temporary.

And yet I was starting to see that the city itself brimmed with hidden treasures, and that my clinging to what I'd known had prohibited me from finding something better.

That summer I rented in Fort Greene, again from a graphic designer. She was a slight person who lived without one comfortable piece of furniture. The chairs were hard plastic, the sofa an Ikea cushion on wood ribs. But I loved walking around and around Fort Greene Park for exercise as the gigantic old trees blossomed.

My husband bought a handmade bowler at Malchijah Hats. Changing the hatband, if you ever wanted to, came free.

"You doing it! You doing it!" exclaimed a man on the street—smiling at my husband's hipster style, but not nastily.

The night before we departed that second apartment, I sat on its brownstone steps. I was stricken again with melancholy. Saying goodbye was both easier than before and just as hard. It's unfair, I protested with childish logic: *I love this, therefore I should get to keep it.* And yet despite myself, the city was teaching me that those treasures I most enjoyed were the ones I could least anticipate because they were devised by people whose personalities had different strengths than mine.

I was learning, too, that surprise was crucial in determining what I might fall in love with. The world was often better than I expected. I didn't have to be so in control all the time, so on guard. Why, even something tiny can cause great pleasure! I recalled the Fort Greene neighbor who wore around her neck a bandana out of which one day poked a brilliant yellow triangle that cried, "Peep! Peep!" "Is that a bird around your neck?" I asked. It was. It had fallen out of its nest, and this woman was nursing it to health. She'd worn it everywhere: on the subway, on her dog-walking jaunts. She showed it to me, opening her bandana further: the plump black glossy grackle body, the gleaming eye above the urgent yellow beak. *See*, I told myself. *You never know what beautiful surprise might come!* Stay put, and you see less. That thought provided some balm as, the next morning, I hauled my suitcase down the stairs.

The third apartment we rented from a composer on Middagh, in Brooklyn Heights. It was a famous tiny street. Carson McCullers had lived here with both Auden and Gypsy Rose Lee while Gypsy wrote *The G-String Murders*, although their house itself had long ago been sacrificed to the BQE. Around the corner from our new digs was an Egyptian café where for $4.50 you could get falafel with pita they cooked on the spot. You ordered, and the man rolled out the dough with a rolling pin. Down the hill was the new Brooklyn Bridge Park, where I found myself standing beside Mayor Bloomberg at a food film festival. I'd had a glass of beer at the festival, and now the mayor manifested himself. "We love you, Mayor Bloomberg," came the voice out of my pleasantly inebriated self. "You're doing a wonderful job!" He looked deeply tanned, as if he'd just arrived from the Bahamas. "Wha'd I do?" he asked, with comic modesty. I said nothing in response, for we had reached the end of my euphoric ability to hobnob with the famous.

Or had we? Because, although he was instantly engulfed by the bleaching lights of a news camera, his question kept rankling. "I wish I'd told him which of his policies I liked," I moaned. I could still see pieces of him amid the throng that now surrounded him. "Get back in there!" exclaimed my husband, propelling me Bloomberg-ward. And then, a miracle! A very tanned hand came through the crowd. The mayor saw me approaching and hauled me in. "You asked me what policies of yours I liked," I said. "And I wanted to tell you." And I did (gun control, calories being posted, the trans fats work; Occupy Wall Street hadn't happened yet or I would have tempered my endorsement).

The moral of which is, I informed myself, that once you head off in the direction you want, unexpected allies often conspire to help you on your way. So why not head off with more lightheartedness? Why pine, I asked as I zipped up my suitcase.

And I was almost convinced.

For by now the rhythm of going away and coming back had come to seem so dazzlingly quick that when I returned to the city, I was no longer disoriented. I picked up right where I'd left off, with just a slight amnesiac stutter in between, as if I were successfully living in more than one place at once, both Texas and New York, both the past and the present and almost the future, as if I were a Piaget child who'd learned the persistence of the beloved even when the beloved is out of sight. And yet—would loss always evoke a tormenting pang? Would that never fully change?

My next-to-last sublet was at the top of a brownstone in Clinton Hill. The owner of the apartment was a cinematographer, and everyone looked glamorous in his rooms. The light was diffuse, silky—no bulb, I soon discovered, was more than 40 watts. My first day I screwed in 100-watt bulbs so I could read, and the lamps remained beautiful but refused to part with their light: their shades were opaque chocolate-brown, although their brass bases glowed like Aladdin lamps. One shone up at a little book tucked on a shelf: *Letters to a Young Artist*, modeled on the famous Rilke book but with missives from contemporary painters and sculptors. I read it on a chair the cinematographer had set beside the window.

"If you want to be a person who can survive on your art, you must clarify what can be exchanged with society before society will repay you," said the installation artist Xu Bing. "I was fearful and panicked . . . but I did it anyway," said Jessica Stockholder, a conceptual artist, talking about taking an important risk.

These were new thoughts for me. I'd always assumed being panicked meant that you were doing the *wrong* thing, and that you ought to wait until you were calm before even contemplating making a change. So I'd actually relinquished the gift of my unhappiness; I'd squandered it, disowned it, telling myself, "Get calm. Don't even think about change until you're no longer upset. After all, you can't think clearly when you're so stirred up!"—and so I'd cast my life in emotional cement for year after year.

I'd remained in relationships too long and worked on projects too long, I saw now, gazing out the window at bustling Washington Avenue. Fear had always meant, to me, *Don't do it!*

And wasn't fear also an aspect of my clinging? After all, what did that pang mean when I left a place? It was mere attachment, in both the psychological and the spiritual sense. And it was the illusion that I would never have the good thing again. It was the illusion that something was wrong *because* I was sad, rather than that nothing was wrong *although* I was sad.

Of course the inevitability of loss is one of the big lessons of the Buddha. It is one of the essential truths, and as long as I tried to shield myself from it, I merely narrowed my life.

I'm writing this from a shockingly quiet apartment in Clinton Hill. Owned by an international journalist, its walls are covered with maps and its bookshelves must hold a hundred guidebooks. I think of it as the Invisible Apartment. It's perched on the roof of a brownstone, an apartment so tiny it can't be seen from the street, and it has no neighbors on any side except beneath its floorboards. When it's time to leave again I know I'll feel that pang, but I no longer feel a need to fight it. It's even a kind of friend.

Life is all a sublet anyway, of course. We don't fully own even the bodies we live in; we can't stop them from changing. We cede them from year to year. And this knowledge of loss, I've discovered, is the salt that brings up the savor of all the rest—understanding that none of it is mine to keep. It's loss that provides the edge that makes the world sharply beautiful. Without it, life would pall; it would be far less intense. The pang is the small price we pay.

I don't think I'll ever get to the level of real detachment—nor do I even seek it. Yet I've had these glimpses, as if I've taken a step back from my own life and can see the glittering pattern, all those scissor moments slicing us away from the past, letting us join the future, and I'm thankful for a perspective that makes the inevitability of change easier to accept.

The Three Marks of Existence

Sylvia Boorstein

Impermanence, suffering, emptiness—these three, said the Buddha, mark all of existence. That could be seen as extremely bad news, and from ego's point of view it is. But the Insight Meditation teacher Sylvia Boorstein says that if we look at these truths with an awakened eye, we will find the good news of joy, resilience, and a deep sense of connection with others.

I was walking through the airport terminal when my eyes met those of a baby approaching me, strapped into a carrier on his mother's chest, and I *knew* that baby was me. A thrill went through me. I knew in that moment it did not matter that I was aging because that baby—*me*, in a newer, fresher guise—was on his way up in life.

I recall laughing, maybe even out loud, as the baby and mother passed by. I knew that the others around me were all me, too, and the mother and baby and each other as well, coming and going in this airline terminal and in life. I felt happy and said to myself, "Thinking about interconnection is one thing, but these moments of direct understanding are great." I sat in the boarding lounge feeling tremendous affection for my fellow travelers.

Such an understanding of interconnection comes, in Buddhist

practice, from awareness of the three characteristics of experience, also known as the three marks of existence. The first is *impermanence*, or as one teacher put it to me, the idea that "last year's Super Bowl is in the same past as the Revolutionary War." The second is *suffering*, which he described as the result of "the mind unable to accommodate its experience."

These two characteristics, or insights, are fairly easy to make sense of, and when I first began my Buddhist practice, I found I had a basic grasp of them. I thought, "Who doesn't know these things?" But the third characteristic, *emptiness*—the insight that there is no enduring self that separates anything from anything else—seemed more elusive to me, and not particularly relevant to my life. I liked the rest of what I was learning and practicing, so I figured I would just let that one alone for now.

The insight about impermanence was, in my early years of practice, what seemed most dramatically evident—although not in a comfortable way. There were periods, especially on retreat, in which it seemed to me that all I could see was the passing away of everything. I saw, as I hadn't ever before, that sunsets followed every dawn and that the beautiful full moon immediately waned. As I came upon a flower that was newly opening, I simultaneously envisioned the wilted look it would have three days hence. I remember tearfully reporting to my teacher, Joseph Goldstein, "It's so sad! Everything is dying!" He responded, "It's not sad, Sylvia. It's just true." I found that calming at the time, but I would say it differently now. I would say, "It's not sad. But it *is* poignant."

Everything has a life cycle, with beauty in every part of it, and the passing of any part of it evokes a response, either of relief or nostalgia. Eighteen-year-olds are usually glad to be finished with adolescence and off to whatever they'll do next. A woman in a class I was teaching recently said her daughter, at that point anticipating her marriage a week hence, was sad that all the excitement of planning and imagining would soon be over forever. An elderly man who once took a seniors' yoga class I was teaching thanked me after the class but said he would not be coming back. "It is too hard for me," he said. "But I would like to tell you that I was a member of the 1918 Olympic rowing team."

I find now that time seems to be speeding up. I've become seventy-five years old in what feels like a brief time. The woman I see when I look in the mirror is my Aunt Miriam. It still startles me, but it also inspires me. Knowing that I have limited time left inspires me not to mortgage any time to negative mind states. I am determined not to miss any day waiting for a better one. "Carpe diem!" has never seemed like a more important injunction.

An immediately helpful aspect of my earliest insights into impermanence was the increased tolerance and courage I experienced in difficult situations. However much I had known intellectually that things pass, more and more I knew it in the marrow of my bones. I responded better to difficult news. Hearing that my father had been diagnosed with an incurable cancer, I felt both deeply saddened and uncharacteristically confident. I thought, "We'll manage this together. We've run 10K races together. We'll do this too." On a more mundane level, I noticed that I was more relaxed about ordinary unpleasantness. "This painful procedure at the dentist is taking very long, but in another hour I'll be out of here."

From the beginning of my practice, the insight about suffering, especially the extra mental tension that compounds the pain of life's inevitable losses, made sense to me. A melancholy boyfriend I had when I was in high school enjoyed reciting Dylan Thomas poetry to me. I found it romantic, in a Brontë kind of way, but also depressing. I definitely thought it would be wrong to "Rage, rage against the dying of the light," and I knew I didn't want to do that. When, years later, I learned about Buddhism's four noble truths, I was particularly inspired by the promise of the fourth noble truth, the path of practice that I thought would assure me of a mind that did not rage.

When I first began to teach, I would explain the four truths this way:

Life is challenging because everything is always changing and we continually need to adjust to new circumstances.

Adding struggle to challenge creates suffering. Pain is inevitable but suffering is optional.

Peace is possible. In the middle of a complicated life, the mind can remain at ease.

The path for developing this kind of mind involves attention to ethical behavior, to disciplining the habits of mind through meditation, and to ardent intention.

I loved the third noble truth, the truth that liberation is possible. I felt that after hearing about the ubiquitous ways that we are challenged—and how heedlessly and habitually we respond to the challenges in unwise ways—it was a great relief to hear, "Peace is possible!" I said it with great conviction and I believed it then and I believe it now. What I've started to add now, out of my own experience, is that however much I know that struggling makes things worse, I still suffer. If I am pained enough, or disappointed enough, or anxious enough, I still suffer.

Some life experiences bring us to our knees. Someone in a class I was once teaching, after I had talked about the intensity of even terrible experiences modulating with time because "everything passes," said, "In my case I think I am going to pass before the horror of this passes." I was humbled by the anguish I heard in what that person said, and it has kept me more real and more honest.

For a while, in an attempt to be honest but lighthearted, I added what I called the third-and-a-half noble truth: that the intention to "surrender to the experience" doesn't necessarily cause it to happen. These days even lightheartedness seems glib to me, so I don't do it anymore. I say, "When the mind is able to surrender to the truth, grieving happens and suffering lessens." But there is no timetable for that to happen, and the only possible response I can have is compassion for myself and for other people. Maybe *that* truth—that we suffer in spite of knowing that peace is possible, and sense it is true for everyone—contributes to our sense of kinship, the sense of feeling like I'm accompanied that I sometimes experience in a crowd of strangers.

The idea of no separate, enduring self—emptiness—*is* a peculiar idea until we have a direct experience of it. It certainly feels that there is a little "Me" living in our bodies that decides what to do, that sees out of our eyes, that realizes it has woken up in the morning. The "Me" has thought patterns that are habitual associated with it, so it feels enduring. If I woke up one morning thinking other people's thoughts, it would be deeply disturbing.

So it was a complete surprise to me, some years into my retreat practice, to be practicing walking meditation, sensing physical movements and sights and smells and heat and cool, and realizing that everything was happening all by itself. No one was taking that walk: "I" wasn't there. I *was* there a few seconds later, recovering my balance after the "uh-oh" feeling of "if no one is here, who is holding me up?" I thought, "This is wild! There really *isn't* anyone in here directing the show. It is all just happening." I understood that the arising of intention causes things to happen, and that intention arises as a result of circumstances such as hearing the instruction, "Do walking meditation." Hearing the instruction was the proximal cause of walking happening. The habit of following instructions, developed since birth, was another cause.

In years since, the understanding that everything anyone does is a result of karma—of causes and effects—has helped to keep me from labeling people as good or bad. Circumstances and behavior can change, of course, but at any given time no one can be other than the sum of all of their contingent causes. A student in a class discussion about this topic once said, "When people ask me, 'How are you?' I always answer, 'I couldn't be better.' Because, I couldn't!"

It's true. We couldn't, any of us, be better. In our most out-of-sorts days, we couldn't be better. If we could, we would. Suffering happens, but no "one" decides to suffer.

As a beginning student, I wondered whether hearing about the three characteristics of experience, rather than discovering them for myself, would diminish their impact—that thinking about them wouldn't count as much as discovering them directly. Today, I know that thinking, pondering, and reflecting on them count as well as direct moments of experience. Everything counts.

MEDITATION: INTERCONNECTEDNESS

Here's a practice that directly evokes the truth that there is no separate and enduring self, meditated on in the context of interconnectedness.

Read these instructions and then sit up or lie down with your spine straight and your body relaxed, so that breath can flow easily in and out of your body. Close your eyes. Don't do anything at all to manipulate or regulate your breathing. Let your experience be like wide-awake sleeping, with breath coming and going at its own rate.

Probably you'll be aware of your diaphragm moving up and down as your chest expands and contracts. Of course you cannot feel that the exhaling air is rich in carbon dioxide and the inhaling air is rich in oxygen, but you probably know that. You also probably know that the green life in the world—the trees and vines and shrubs and grasses—are breathing in carbon dioxide and releasing oxygen back into the environment. The green world and your lungs, as long as they both are viable, are keeping each other alive.

Without any volition on your part, your body is part of the world happening, and the world is part of your body continuing. Nothing is separate. Your life is part of all life. Where is the self?

Booooring . . .

Karen Maezen Miller

Chögyam Trungpa Rinpoche called the experience of meditation "cool boredom"—when our fears and hopes and discursiveness subside and we are content simply to be present. We could be staring at a wall. Or counting our breaths. Or living life just as it is. Zen teacher Karen Maezan Miller here extols the virtues of boredom.

The message comes with good intentions, as do most things designed to inspire, so I click on the link in my e-mail and watch the short video.

First I see a sleeping newborn swaddled in a blanket, followed by a silken black butterfly perched on a finger, a dewdrop dangling from a leaf tip, and a nest cradling two luminous robin eggs. Images dissolve to a piano serenade—a foggy meadow at daybreak, the fiery blaze of an ocean sunset, a peach pie cooling on a plank table, and a vase of peonies gracing a windowsill. A boy bites a glistening red Popsicle at that perfect instant before it slides off the stick. A golden-haired girl blows the dancing flames from her birthday candles. "Moments," the voiceover says. "Moments like this are all we have."

They are happy, captivating shots, drenched in color and sentiment. The eye wants to drink them in and dwell. Compared to this, my life seems mostly washed-out and even wasted.

I stop the show. Something's wrong with this picture. Pies and Popsicles are appealing, but these pictures don't quite capture the essence of life. Not the whole of it.

Later on, in the bathroom picking up dingy wet towels, I notice the mildew creeping up the bottom of the shower curtain. This is not the life of precious tributes. It's not one of the moments you want to frame and keep. It's one you want to throw out. And many of us do. We replace people, places, and things that have grown charmless and tiresome—which they always do. Fascination fades and restlessness stirs.

Chasing the picture-perfect, we can lose what we have in abundance—the times that teach us even more than the rare delight of butterflies or a robin's blue eggs. We lose the hours, the days, and the decades when nothing much seems to happen at all. Time freezes. Paint dries. Mildew spreads. We're bored out of our minds.

Boredom is the unappreciated path to patience, peace, and intimacy, so who would read a paean to it? Let that be your koan.

FACE THE WALL

Bodhidharma faced the wall.

The Second Ancestor of Zen, having cut off his arm, stood there in the snow and said, "My mind is not at peace yet. I beg you, Master, please put it to rest."

Bodhidharma said, "Bring me your mind, and I will put it to rest."

The Second Ancestor said, "I have searched for my mind, but I cannot take hold of it."

Bodhidharma said, "There, I have put your mind to rest."

I happen to love this koan. Every time I look at it I notice something beautiful. You might not see it, because there's not much going on here. Plus it doesn't paint an especially pretty picture. One guy faces the wall. Another one stands frozen in a colorless landscape, going stir-crazy.

It's the crazy part I relate to.

Bring Me Your Boredom

"I'm bored."

Schoolchildren can be afflicted with it by the second day of summer; workers by the sixth month on the job; spouses by the seventh year of marriage; and readers by the tenth paragraph. Or before.

Are you bored yet? Nowadays, boredom is considered a scourge. We blame boredom for the death of curiosity, learning, productivity, innovation, and commitment. Boredom is the antecedent to all kinds of distractions, disengagements, overindulgences, and infidelities. The worst crime is being boring, the joke goes, but we all know that the real crimes are likely to come after. In the name of boredom, we overfill our minds, our bodies, our senses, and our time. We flee what fails to amuse. Boredom breeds contempt, and contempt breeds calamity.

If boredom is such a menace, let's bring it out into the open. Can you show it to me? Like the other thoughts and feelings we use to torment ourselves, boredom is something we can't locate except in our own deadly pronouncement: "I'm bored." By the time we say it, we believe it, and believing is all it takes. This is where the story can get interesting.

When we're bored, we go looking for something new. And let's face it: we're nearly always looking for something new. It doesn't matter how much or how little we've got—how well we each manage our store of talents or prospects—we are somehow convinced that we haven't yet got "it," not enough to be completely satisfied or secure. We might think we need something as harmless as a cookie, a game, or a gadget—or another career, lover, or child. We might call what we want higher purpose, wisdom, passion, or simply a change of scenery.

Until we are at peace with ourselves, the quest continues. Until we know that there is nowhere else to go, and nothing more to get, we are trapped in delusion. We cannot resolve delusion with more delusion, but we try, and in the search we drive ourselves further away from reality and into raving madness. Fighting boredom is a full-time occupation.

What does it take to liberate ourselves from the chase? What if we could release the grasping mind that is always clawing after some precious new thing, even if it's only a new fantasy? That would be excruciating, or so we fear. It's the fear of letting go that afflicts us, but letting go is pain-free.

SEARCH THE MIND

One time I was interviewed by a radio host about meditation, and she seemed alarmed, even offended, by the idea. Staying put runs contrary to the religion of self-gratification.

"It seems to me you're telling people to settle," she said. I was flummoxed, and I searched my mind for a response. If I'd had the equanimity of my Zen forebears, I would have said what I really meant.

I would have said, "Yes."

What's wrong with settling? What's wrong with being patient and making peace? What's wrong with quieting the crazy-making, egocentric mind? And for that matter, what's wrong with boredom? It's not the feeling of boredom that hurts us; it's what we do when we try to run away from it.

If we find one thing boring, we'll find everything boring, so we'd better learn to look at boredom differently. We'd better see things as they really are. This is why we begin our practice, and this is why we keep practicing even when we are no longer entertained. If we are really committed, we can indeed bore ourselves out of our ruminating mind and into a world at rest.

In the Soto Zen tradition, we meditate with our eyes slightly open, facing a blank wall. Like Bodhidharma, who was said to have faced the wall for nine years before his first student appeared in the snowdrifts, we are called wall gazers. People often ask about the meaning of the wall, since it seems so extreme, or at the very least, extremely boring.

It's true; sometimes the wall we face is a bare white wall, where we are looking at nothing. This wall is called a wall. At other times, we turn around and face another kind of wall, where we are looking at everything. This wall is called the world. There always seems to be a wall of some kind or another in front of us; the question is whether or not we can face it.

Whatever the scenery, our practice is the same. Our practice is to face everything life is, and everything it isn't. Everything we think and feel, and everything we don't. Wall gazing is a very thorough practice in facing the fleetingness of things and not getting trapped in momentary apparitions. All apparitions, it turns out, are momentary. When your eyes are open and you are intimately engaged with what appears in front of you, it's hard to stay bored because nothing stays one way for long. Even walls disappear.

When my husband comes home, he asks me what happened during the day.

There were no piano serenades at my house. No misty meadows or fiery sunsets. No newborns. No birthdays. I did not make a pie. It was a day like any other that can bore you out of your mind.

"Nothing," I say.

But that doesn't mean I'm bored. I have been facing the wall where the snow falls, paint dries, towels fade, and mildew spreads—the same wall where the light blooms in a continuous spectacle of color, sensation, and imagery that is the undivided whole of life. I have been practicing the equanimity of my Zen forebears, but even now I have not said what I really mean when I say, "Nothing."

I mean, "Everything."

What could ever be wrong with this picture?

Playing with Buddha

Ira Sukrungruang

"The Buddha is with you," his mother used to say. "Believe in him." At age seven, Ira Sukrungruang believed that the Buddha was more than a bronze statue. The Buddha was his best friend.

I used to stare at the meditating Buddha in our living room: his straight-backed posture, his wide shoulders and narrow waist, his elegant hands resting humbly in his lap. This statue sat on a shelf seven feet high. Around him were other Buddhas, two yellow candles, and a cup of rice to hold incense sticks. He could rest comfortably in my palm and weighed no more than a couple of pounds. Yet he was heavy in spiritual weight, my father always said.

The Buddha, like my mother and father, was not native to America. He had been in my family for years, ever since my father was a barefoot boy running wildly in Ayutthaya, Thailand. I wondered if the Buddha, too, felt misplaced in this new world—a world without the heat and humidity of his native home, without the familiar sounds of geckos and mynahs and the evening song of croaking frogs. This was America. This was Illinois. This was Chicago. Here, the house shook on Mondays when the garbage truck rumbled by. Here, our neighbor Jack rode endless loops on his riding lawn mower.

My family revolved around the Buddha. Each morning, before

I went to school, I prayed to him. Some days, my mother allowed me to stand on a dining-room chair to offer him a shot glass of coffee—cream, no sugar. Other days, she let me light the candles and incense before we prayed. I was supposed to close my eyes and think only good thoughts, but my eyes remained open, fixed on the Buddha. I imagined that, at any moment, he would rise and float down like an autumn leaf. I imagined he would impart vital secrets, and I could ask him the questions that plagued me. There, in the living room, he would walk onto the palms of my hands and we would spend the evening—boy and Buddha—speaking like friends.

"The Buddha is with you," my mother used to say. "Believe in him."

And so I believed that the Buddha was more than a bronze statue, that he was solid like a body is solid—the way it gives a bit when you lean against it, the way it molds to accept the presence of another. He possessed the gift of language and was bilingual like me, skipping freely between English and Thai. We spoke often, our conversations in hushed whispers, and he sounded soothing, not harsh like my elementary school principal or gargled like the monks at temple. Buddha was the holder of my secrets. He understood that loneliness and emptiness were one and the same.

Once, when I was in the living room, my mother asked from the kitchen who I was talking to.

"Buddha," I told her.

"Excellent," she said. "Speak to him every day, okay?"

Mrs. Slusarchak, my second-grade teacher, asked my mother to come for a meeting one afternoon.

A patient teacher, Mrs. S lived in Munster, Indiana. "I live in Munster," she always said, "like the stinky cheese." But I thought she was saying "monster," and I imagined hairy demons living in cheese-shaped houses. I liked her. She wore bright dresses—Hawaiian pastels—that seemed to ward off the dreary Chicago winter days. She looked pretty with her short hair and small glasses and laughed with her whole body, which was shocking but funny.

The day of the meeting, my mother came straight from work, still in her nurse's uniform. She smiled timidly, her purse in her lap, and sat across from Mrs. S. I was next to my mother, but I aimed my eyes out the window at the swing set.

Mrs. S said that I was a math champ every week and that my penmanship was the best in the class. My mother patted my head and said, "We practice every day."

"I can tell," Mrs. S said, then let out a laugh that nearly knocked my mother off the chair. "But I'm concerned about his behavior."

"Has he been bad?" my mother said. "I will tell him to be better."

Mrs. S shook her head. "Not in the least. He's just terribly shy."

She went on to talk about what had happened at recess. How I'd wanted to get on the swing but Tommy W told me to go away, so I did and sat on the bench, staring at my hands. This was what I did often, she said. Stare at my hands. I could never meet her eyes. I could never speak more than two words at a time. "There are days," she said, "that I don't hear a word from him."

"Is this true?" my mother asked me in Thai.

I stared at my hands and my mother sighed. It was a sigh that said she knew exactly what Mrs. S was talking about. "I'm sorry for him," she said. "He is like me." She, too, had a fear that gripped her. It made her hide in her room, reading magazines and sewing endless dresses she would never wear.

Mrs. S nodded. She understood. She suggested my mother enroll me in Cub Scouts or other activities, so that I would be encouraged to meet some friends. My mother agreed, and the next day she sent me to school with a bagful of apples for my teacher.

But what I wanted to say was that I had a friend: Buddha. And within him was a heart that beat strong and that awakened something in me.

This was not a spiritual awakening—not a recognition beyond the self as many theologians would define it. Nor was it a sudden epiphany to a transcendent crisis. I was too young to comprehend such lofty ideas, too young to fully understand what Buddhism was or why my family was so devoted to it. I was being awakened in the way a newborn registers it has fingers and toes, and those fingers and toes have function. I was being awakened in the same way you realize that if you see one bird, you might see another and another. You realize that you are not as alone as you thought you were. The world is filled with birds, or in this case, with buddhas, and every buddha is a friend.

"I spoke to him every day," my friend told me. "His name was Bob." My friend and I were in our early twenties, and in the best place to be on a hot summer evening in Chicago—an over-air-conditioned bar. He was relaying tales of the imaginary friend he had when he lived clear across the ocean, growing up in a semi-affluent family in Poland.

"What did you two talk about?" I asked.

"Bob was well-versed in all subjects."

We laughed. "Do you remember when he started appearing?" I said.

"About the time when my mom was about to ditch my dad and come here."

"You think that's why Bob appeared?" Imaginary friends, I'd discovered through research, often materialize during stressful moments in a child's life. It is how the child grasps and copes with the turmoil of his or her situation.

My friend shrugged and seemed to speak more to his drink than to me. "I remember what Bob looked like, though." Then he went on to describe Bob, who had crazy wild hair that went in all directions and who always appeared barefoot and in a blue-and-white-striped sweater and khaki shorts. "Isn't that crazy?" he said.

I shook my head.

"What's crazier," said my friend, "is that I thought I saw him the other day. At work."

"An older Bob or young Bob?

"The same Bob."

"Was he barefoot?" I asked.

"Can't be barefoot in Home Depot. But he had on the same sweater and he was holding hands with his dad."

"Are you sure it was Bob?" I asked.

"Nope." My friend ordered another drink. "When you talk about imaginary friends, you really can't be sure of anything."

Maybe I can't be sure of Buddha. But I am sure that when I was seven I was picked on and bullied. I am sure that I was born an only child and spent much of my time by myself. I am sure that I am the son of two immigrant parents who loved me with all their being, even more than they loved each other, and sometimes, because of this love, they smothered me with suffocating affection. I am sure that my family was scared and they, too, turned to Buddha for day-to-day guidance through this world that was not Thailand, where it snowed when there should have been hot, devouring sun. I am sure that I possessed an overactive imagination. I am sure that when I felt overwhelmed, I hid myself within the darkness of my arms and made the world sound hollow like a cave. I am sure that the safest place in the world when I was small was the back of my mother's knees. I am sure that the mind is a mysterious muscle, and the mind of a child is even more mysterious.

And of this I am positive: every time I looked at the Buddha in the living room, I found myself calm, serene, as if caught in a moment before waking or sleeping.

Before I went to sleep, I talked to Buddha. My parents were trying to reclaim their bedroom. Up until then, I'd wedged myself between them on their handmade bed. I was a husky boy and prone to tossing and turning. When I was three or four, this was fine, but now I possessed a larger body that took up more of the bed, and my father was tired of having my hand slapping his face.

At night my new room scared me, even though my mother and father had painted it the light shade of green I'd asked for, and even though I'd been in it countless times during the day. Darkness changed the landscape of the room. There was an absence of color, and that absence felt oppressive. The only furniture was a twin bed and a metal desk, and there was nothing on the walls, except for a small Buddha pendant hanging above the bed and a picture of my father when he was a monk. Although it was only half the size of my parents', my room seemed too big, sonorous. I felt there were places for monsters to hide, especially in the closet, and I convinced myself there were things that existed in there. Unpleasant things.

I frequently ended up back in my parents' bed until my father put his foot down. "Big boys sleep in their own rooms," he said. "You are a big boy, yes?"

I nodded.

"Nothing can hurt you," he said. "Buddha protects us."

And he did. He sat cross-legged on my bed, not in a meditating fashion, but how I sat when Mrs. S read to us. My Buddha did not speak sage advice. He adopted schoolyard lingo, and told me the kids at school were dork noses and that I was much better than they were. At night, Buddha eased me to sleep with his wild stories. "One time," he'd begin, and the tale would take off in bizarre and outrageous directions, always ending with a hero who stood tall and was not afraid to take on the world. We played rock, paper, scissors, and Buddha was always shocked when I beat him. Then when the darkest part of the night came, he hovered above me and I could feel the heat of his presence. His skin glowed, like a night-light.

One day imaginary friends are there and the next they are not. This is true of real friends, also. The friends we had when we were in school—what happened to them? Jody is now a photographer in North Carolina. Casey works for USAA in Texas. Andrea is a schoolteacher in Illinois. What we share is a past, a period in time. We become a memory. We become part of a sentence that begins with, "Remember Ira . . . "

But seldom do we remember our imagined friends, because to admit to them is to somehow admit to a deficiency on our part. Yet they existed, too. They were essential. But now we want to keep our friends a secret—to protect them from ridicule, from sideways glances. They protected us when we were younger, and now it's our turn to protect them.

"Remember Buddha?" I want to say. "Dude told the craziest stories."

Before Buddha became Buddha, he was a boy. He was Prince Siddhartha, heir to his father's throne, groomed to be the greatest king to ever live. This was the pressure he lived with day in, day out. I imagine this to be stifling, every limb weighed down with lead. I imagine that even Siddhartha, a boy destined for greatness, might crumble under that pressure. And the king sensed it, too. He feared his son would leave the palace, so he built other palaces within the palace; there would be no need for Siddhartha to leave. But what does a boy do without others around him?

I wondered about this.

As soon as I learned how to read, my mother gave me a book entitled *The Story of Buddha*. It was published by a press in New Delhi in 1978 and had pictures on every other page. What I remember most about the book were the times Siddhartha spent alone, something that displeased his father. The king bemoaned his son's lack of interest in his education as a king. He complained how Siddhartha would rather be alone in the garden than with his teachers. But was he alone? Did he speak to the butterflies, the birds, the critters that scampered around in green? Could Siddhartha, who possessed an extraordinary mind, have imagined someone in that garden with him, someone to assuage his loneliness?

Possibly.

Later, when Siddhartha became Buddha, he would teach us that nothing is ever truly alone; everything is in relation to everything else.

God is in everything. He is everywhere. He is always with you. Sitting with my wife's family at their Presbyterian church, I often hear these words, which are not dissimilar to the ones I heard when I was a boy sitting in temple listening to a monk's sermon. *Buddha is with you. Keep him in your mind and heart.* We look to these spiritual guides for ways to calm our tumultuous lives. There is comfort in the notion that we are never alone, that we are connected by an invisible thread to everything else in the world, the seen and the unseen.

Buddha remained unseen when I traveled down the stairs in a laundry basket, one of my favorite games. But he was there, sitting with me. He remained unseen when we wrestled with body pillows. But he was there, with a pulverizing elbow. He remained unseen when I played with my action figures. But he was there, making my GI Joes move in combative maneuvers. He remained unseen when I played football outside. But he was there, my wide receiver, catching passes for touchdowns.

The real Buddha would not do such things. The real Buddha would have preached peace and emphasized the life of the mind. But my Buddha was a mix of wisdom and mischief. He was my friend, after all, and as friends we were on equal ground.

This friendship, this very idea of Buddha, made me change, if only a little. It made me yearn for real companionship, and perhaps that was the reason I fought against my shyness. If I could speak to Buddha, why couldn't I speak to the weird boy with the spiked hair who looked just as lonely as I was? Or the other boy with the golden hair and thick glasses? Or the other boy who was as gangly as a bean? Perhaps they had imaginary friends, too, and in this we shared something. Perhaps our imaginary friends would not be needed anymore, and they would simply disappear.

At what moment my imaginary friend disappeared, I don't remember. But he did, and so did the Buddha on the shelf one evening when I was a teenager. Then there was a new Buddha, a green one made of jade and covered in sparkling gold robes. This new Buddha was beautiful the way something new is beautiful, but I found myself looking for the familiar tarnish, the layer of dust that blanketed the old Buddha. The old Buddha went when my father went; it was his, after all, and was one of the only things he took with him after the divorce.

I missed that old Buddha, my friend—missed his presence, his watchful gaze on the shelf. There were questions I still wanted to ask, guidance I still sought. I wonder what the view is like where he is now, and does he remember the boy who used to talk to him? He sat there for fifteen years of my life, and though Buddha has become Buddha again and not my play pal, he is never far from my mind. All I have to do is close my eyes to see him: his straight-backed posture, his wide shoulders and narrow waist, his elegant hands resting humbly in his lap.

Good Citizens: Creating Enlightened Society

Thich Nhat Hanh

If humanity is going to have the kind of future we hope for, we will need to profoundly change the way we live and relate to each other. Economics, politics, science, psychology—none of these alone offers us the path forward that life on a crowded Earth demands. Only genuine spiritual practice will create the real change we need—in our hearts, minds, and society. Here, the great teacher Thich Nhat Hanh offers us his Buddhist-inspired vision for the enlightened society we all aspire to.

The world in which we live is globalized. Economies halfway around the world affect our own. Our politics, education, and cultural consumption happen on a global scale. Our ethics and morality also need to be globalized. A new global order calls for a new global ethic. A global ethic is the key to addressing the true difficulties of our time.

Around the world, we are facing climate change, terrorism, and wars between people of different religions. Fanaticism, discrimination, division, violence, economic crises, and the destruction of the environment affect us all. We have to look deeply into these sufferings so we can make good decisions and conduct ourselves wisely.

We have to sit down together, as people of many traditions, to find the causes of global suffering. If we look deeply with clarity, calm, and peace, we can see the causes of our suffering, uproot and transform them, and find a way out.

A Global Offering

We are many different cultures and nations, each with its own values, ways of behaving, and criteria for ethical conduct. Every country and every culture can offer something beautiful. It will take all of our collective wisdom to make a global code of ethics. With insight from all the world's people and traditions, we can create a global ethic that is based on mutual respect.

Some people base their ethics on their religion. If you believe there is a deity that decides what is right and wrong regardless of what you observe, then you only need to follow the rules laid out by that religion to engage in right action. Others follow a scientific or utilitarian approach, looking only at what is a logical consequence of their actions. A Buddhist contribution to global ethics is different from both of these. It is based on observing and understanding the world with mindfulness, concentration, and insight. It begins with an awareness of the nonduality of subject and object, and the interconnectedness of all things. It is a practice that can be accepted by everyone, regardless of whether or not you believe in a god. When you train yourself in this practice, you will see that you have more freedom.

Applying Buddhist Ethics in Daily Life

We created the term "engaged Buddhism" during the Vietnam War. As monks, nuns, and laypeople during the war, many of us practiced sitting and walking meditation. But we would hear the bombs falling around us, and the cries of the children and adults who were wounded. To meditate is to be aware of what is going on. What was going on around us was the suffering of many people and the destruction of life. So we were motivated by the desire to do something to relieve the suffering within us and around us. We wanted to serve others and we wanted to practice sitting and walking meditation to give us the stability and peace we needed to go out of the temple and help relieve this suffering. We walked mindfully right alongside suffering, in the places where people were still running under the bombs. We practiced mindful breathing as we cared for children wounded by guns or bombs. If we hadn't practiced while we served, we would have lost ourselves, become burned-out, and we would not have been able to help anyone.

Engaged Buddhism was born from this difficult situation; we wanted to maintain our practice while responding to the suffering around us. Engaged Buddhism isn't just Buddhism that's involved in social problems. Engaged Buddhism means we practice mindfulness wherever we are, whatever we are doing, at any time. When we are alone, walking, sitting, drinking our tea, or making our breakfast, that can also be engaged Buddhism. We practice this way not only for ourselves but also to preserve ourselves so that we are able to help others and be connected with all life. Engaged Buddhism is not just self-help. It helps us feel stronger and more stable and also more connected to others and committed to the happiness of all beings.

Engaged Buddhism is Buddhism that penetrates into life. If Buddhism is not engaged, it's not real Buddhism. This is the attitude of the bodhisattvas, beings whose whole intention and actions are to relieve suffering. We practice meditation and mindfulness not only for ourselves; we practice to relieve the suffering of all beings and of the Earth itself. With the insight of interbeing—that we are inherently interconnected with all other beings—we know that when other people suffer less, we suffer less. And when we suffer less, other people suffer less.

Now, as well as engaged Buddhism, we are using the term "applied Buddhism." "Applied" is a word that is often used in science, and we deliberately use it here as a way of saying that our understanding of reality can be used to help clarify and find a way to transform every situation. In Buddhism, there is something that can be used in every circumstance to shed light on the situation and help solve the problem. There is a way to handle every situation with compassion and understanding so that suffering can be lessened. That is the essence of applied Buddhism.

THE STARTING POINT

Mindfulness is the basis of a Buddhist ethic. What does being mindful mean? It means, first of all, that we stop and observe deeply what is happening in the present moment. If we do this, we can see the suffering that is inside us and around us. We can practice looking deeply with concentration in order to see the causes of this suffering. We need to understand suffering in order to know what kind of action we can take to relieve it. We can use the insight of others, the mindfulness of our *sangha*—our larger community of practitioners—to share our insight and understand what kind of action can lead to the transformation of that suffering. When we have collective insight, it will help us see the mutually beneficial path that will lead to the cessation of suffering, not only for one person, but for all of us.

THE VIRTUOUS PATH

In Vietnamese, we translate "ethics" as *dao duc*, the virtuous path. *Duc* means virtue in the sense of honesty, integrity, and understanding. The word is small but it implies a lot—forgiveness, compassion, tolerance, and a sense of common humanity—all the good things that everyone needs. The path should be able to provide the kind of virtuous conduct that will help us to transform and to bring a happy life to everyone. When we have the characteristics of someone who is virtuous, we don't make people suffer. This kind of virtue offers us a guideline, a way of behaving that doesn't cause suffering to others or to ourselves.

Another way to translate "ethics" is *luong li*, which means the behavior of humans to each other. *Luong* means the morality of humans and *li* means the basic principles that lead to correct behavior and correct action. When you put the two phrases together, you get *dao li luong thuong*, which means moral behavior that everyone agrees to. *Thuong* means common, ordinary, something everybody can accept, about which there's a consensus. Ethics are something consistent; they don't change from day to day. So this means a kind of permanent ethics, basic principles we can agree upon that lead to more understanding and acceptance.

MINDFULNESS, CONCENTRATION, AND INSIGHT

From the time of his first teaching delivered to his first disciples, the Buddha was very clear and practical about how we can transform our difficulties, both individually and collectively. He focused on how we put the teachings into practice in our everyday lives. That is ethics. Practice is key because practice generates mindfulness, concentration, and insight. These three energies are the foundation of all Buddhist practice and Buddhist ethics.

We cannot speak about Buddhist ethics without speaking of these three energies. Mindfulness, concentration, and insight help us build a path that will lead to peace and happiness, transformation and healing. It is so important that we don't focus on ethics in the abstract. Our basic practice is the practice of generating the energy of mindfulness, concentration, and insight. We rely on our insight to guide us and help us bring compassion, understanding, harmony, and peace to ourselves and to the world.

Recently, a Christian theologian asked me how to bring about a global spirituality. The person who interviewed me seemed to distinguish between the spiritual and the ethical, but there is always a relationship between the two. Anything can be spiritual. When I pick up my tea in mindfulness, when I look at my tea mindfully, and begin to drink my tea in mindfulness, tea drinking becomes very spiritual. When I brush my teeth in mindfulness, aware that it's wonderful to have the time to enjoy brushing my teeth, aware that

I'm alive, aware that the wonders of life are all around me, and aware that I can brush with love and joy, then tooth-brushing becomes spiritual. When you go to the toilet, defecating or urinating, if you are mindful, this can also be very spiritual.

So there's a deep link between the ethical and the spiritual. If you can't see the spiritual in the ethical, your ethics may be empty. You may live by this ethical code but you don't know why, and so you can't enjoy it. If your ethical and spiritual practices are connected, you will be able to follow your ethical path and be nourished by it.

THE BUDDHA'S FIRST TEACHING

Hundreds of years ago, under a sacred fig tree in Bodh Gaya, India, the Buddha woke up; he realized deep awakening. His first thought upon awakening was the realization that every living being has this capacity to wake up. He wanted to create a path that would help others realize insight and enlightenment. The Buddha did not want to create a religion. To follow a path you don't have to believe in a creator.

After the Buddha was enlightened, he enjoyed sitting under the Bodhi tree, doing walking meditation along the banks of the Neranjara River, and visiting a nearby lotus pond. The children from nearby Uruvela village would come to visit him. He sat and ate fruit with them and gave them teachings in the form of stories. He wanted to share his experience of practice and awakening with his closest five friends and old partners in practice. He heard they were now living in the Deer Park near Benares. It took him about two weeks to walk from Bodh Gaya to the Deer Park. I imagine that he enjoyed every step.

In his very first teaching to his five friends, the Buddha talked about the path of ethics. He said that the path to insight and enlightenment was the noble eightfold path, also called the eight ways of correct practice. The eightfold path is the fourth of the Buddha's four noble truths. If we understand the four noble truths and use their insight to inform our actions in our daily lives, then we are on the path to peace and happiness.

A Path to Action

The four noble truths are the foundation of Buddhism's contribution to a global ethic. These truths are: ill-being exists; there are causes of ill-being; ill-being can be overcome; there is a path to the cessation of ill-being.

The four noble truths, including the noble eightfold path contained in the fourth noble truth, are the Buddha's strategy for handling and relieving suffering. The truths are called "noble," *arya* in Sanskrit, because they lead to the end of suffering. The four noble truths are about suffering, but they are also about happiness. Suffering exists, and we can do something to relieve the suffering within us and around us. Happiness, transformation, and healing are possible. These truths encourage us to act in order to create the happiness we want. They offer an ethical path to our own transformation.

Nonduality

If happiness is possible, why does the Buddha talk first about suffering and ill-being? Why doesn't he just speak about happiness and the path leading to happiness? The Buddha starts with suffering because he knew that happiness and suffering are linked to each other. They inter-are. Suffering contains happiness. Happiness contains suffering. Suffering can be useful. It can teach us the compassion and understanding that are necessary for insight and happiness.

Happiness and suffering are not opposites. This kind of nondualistic thinking is one of the key elements of a Buddhist contribution to a global ethic. The good is not possible without the bad. Good exists because bad exists. The Buddha taught that good and bad are products of our minds, not objective realities. There are many pairs of opposites like this, such as being and nonbeing. We tend to think that being is the opposite of nonbeing. We can't have the notion of being unless we have the notion of nonbeing. We can't have the notion of left without the notion of right. But in fact, reality transcends both being and nonbeing. Being and nonbeing are simply notions; they are two sides of the same reality.

Consider the left and the right. You cannot eliminate the right and keep only the left. Imagine you have a pencil and you are determined to eliminate the right side of the pencil by cutting it in half. As soon as you have thrown one half away, the cut end of the piece that remains becomes the new right. Wherever there is left, there is right. The same is true with good and evil. The notion of goodness and the notion of evil are born from each other. Reality transcends the notions of good and evil.

Subject and object are another pair of opposites. We tend to think of our consciousness as something inside us and the world as something outside. We assume that subject and object exist independently of each other. But subject and object are not separate. They give rise to each other. Reality transcends both. If we observe reality over time and truly taste the teaching of nonduality, we have right understanding.

Once we have this view, the first aspect of the noble eightfold path, then the other aspects of the path easily follow. Right thinking, right speech, right action, right livelihood, right diligence, right mindfulness, and right concentration all arise when we have right view. The Buddhist contribution to a global ethic contains no dogmas. It doesn't say that it is right and everything else is wrong. This understanding is what the Buddha discovered from deep practice and deep observation. We each need to practice mindfulness and deep observation so that we can know the truth for ourselves and not just follow someone else's teaching.

EACH TRUTH CONTAINS THE OTHERS

The nondual nature of reality is also part of the four noble truths. Although there are four truths, each truth contains the others; they can't be considered completely separately from each other. If you fully understand one noble truth, you understand all four. If you really begin to understand suffering, you are already beginning to understand the path to its cessation. The four truths inter-are. Each one contains the others.

The first noble truth is ill-being. The second noble truth is the causes of ill-being, the thoughts and actions that put us on the path leading to ill-being. The third noble truth is well-being, the cessation of ill-being. The fourth noble truth is the path leading to well-being, the noble eightfold path.

The second noble truth is the action that leads to suffering, and the fourth noble truth is the action that leads to well-being, so in a sense they are two pairs of cause and effect. The second noble truth (the path of ill-being) leads us to the first (ill-being), and the fourth noble truth (the noble eightfold path) leads us to the third (well-being, the cessation of ill-being). Either we are walking the noble path or we are on the ignoble path that brings suffering to ourselves and others. We are always on one path or the other.

Mindful Breathing

The four noble truths can't simply be understood intellectually. They contain key ideas, such as nonduality, emptiness, no-self, interbeing, and signlessness, that can only be understood through practice. The foundational practice of the Buddha is mindful breathing. Before we can commit to or practice any ethical action, we need to begin with our breath. Awareness of our breath is the first practical ethical action available to us. This is the only way we can begin to truly understand the basic suffering of human beings and how we might transform it.

When we look at all the suffering around us, at poverty, violence, or climate change, we may want to solve these things immediately. We want to do something. But to do something effectively and ethically, we need to be our best selves in order to be able to handle the suffering.

Being able to stop, to breathe, and to walk or move in mindfulness are the keys to the practice. They can be done anywhere, at any time. We can say:

> Breathing in, I know this is my in-breath.
> Breathing out, I know this is my out-breath.

It's very simple, but very effective. When we bring our attention to our in-breath and our out-breath, we stop thinking of the past, we stop thinking of the future, and we begin to come home to ourselves. Coming home to ourselves is the first thing we need to do, even for politicians, scientists, or economists. Don't think this practice doesn't apply to you. If we don't go home to ourselves, we can't be at our best and serve the world in the best way. We have to be ourselves to be our best. Our quality of being is the foundation for the quality of our actions.

> Breathing in, I'm aware of my whole body.
> Breathing out, I'm aware of my whole body.

Breathing mindfully brings us back to our bodies. We have to acknowledge our bodies first because tension and suffering accumulate in the body. Breathing in this way, we create a kind of family reunion between mind and body. The mind becomes an embodied mind.

If we are truly aware, we know there is tension and pain in our bodies. We can't do our best if we don't know how to release the tension and the pain in ourselves.

> Breathing in, I'm aware of tension in my body.
> Breathing out, I release all the tension in my body.

We can do something right away to improve ourselves and release our tension and suffering so we can see and act more clearly. With our mindful breathing, body and mind come together, established in the here and now, and we can more easily handle the difficult situations in our lives. Mindful breathing brings more well-being into our bodies. In one breath we can recognize and release the tension within us.

We can use our in-breath and out-breath to help us notice the painful feelings inside us. With our in-breath we can acknowledge these feelings and with our out-breath we can let them go.

> Breathing in, I am aware of a painful feeling arising.
> Breathing out, I release the painful feeling.

This is a nonviolent and gentle way to help our bodies release tension and pain.

It is possible to practice mindful breathing in order to produce a feeling of joy, a feeling of happiness. When we are well-nourished and know how to create joy, then we are strong enough to handle the deep pain within ourselves and the world.

With one in-breath and out-breath, we can practice all the four noble truths: we acknowledge our tension or pain and call it by its true name; we release it and let well-being arise.

Living Beautifully with Uncertainty and Change

Pema Chödrön

The essence of the Mahayana Buddhist path is bodhichitta, *often translated as "awakened heart/mind." What awakens the heart? It is love and compassion for all beings, and the intention to put their welfare before our own. One who has this intention is called a bodhisattva, and we can actually become one. The renowned American Buddhist teacher Pema Chödrön shows us how to do it.*

Compassion is threatening to the ego. We might think of it as something warm and soothing, but actually it's very raw. When we set out to support other beings, when we go so far as to stand in their shoes, when we aspire to never close down to anyone, we quickly find ourselves in the uncomfortable territory of "life not on my terms." The commitment traditionally known as the bodhisattva vow, or warrior vow, challenges us to dive into these noncozy waters and swim out beyond our comfort zone. We vow to move consciously into the pain of the world in order to help alleviate it. It is, in essence, a vow to take care of one another, even if it sometimes means not liking how that feels.

This commitment is connected deeply and unshakably with *bodhichitta*, traditionally defined as a longing to awaken so that we can help others do the same, a longing to go beyond the limits of conventional happiness, beyond enslavement to success and failure, praise and blame.

Bodhichitta is also a trust in our innate ability to go beyond bias, beyond prejudice and fixed opinions, and open our hearts to everyone: those we like, those we don't like, those we don't even notice, those we may never meet. Bodhichitta counteracts our tendency to stay stuck in very narrow thinking. It counteracts our resistance to change.

This degree of openness arises from the trust that we all have basic goodness and that we can interact with one another in ways that bring that out. Instead of reacting aggressively when we're provoked, endlessly perpetuating the cycle of pain, we trust that we can engage with others from a place of curiosity and caring and in that way contact their innate decency and wisdom.

Someone sent me a poem that seems to capture the essence of the warrior commitment. Called "Birdfoot's Grampa," the poem is about a boy and his grandfather who are driving on a country road in a rainstorm. The grandfather keeps stopping the car and getting out to scoop up handfuls of toads that are all over the road and then deposit them safely at the roadside. After the twenty-fourth time he's done this, the boy loses patience and tells his grandfather, "You can't save them all / accept it, get back in / we've got places to go." And the grandfather, knee-deep in wet grass, his hands full of toads, just smiles at his grandson and says, "they have places to go to / too."

What a clear illustration of how the commitment to care for all beings everywhere works. The grandfather didn't mind stopping for the twenty-fourth time, didn't mind getting wet to save the toads. He also didn't mind the impatience of his grandson, because he was very clear in his mind that the toads had as much desire to live as he did.

The aspiration of this commitment is huge. But whether we're

making it for the very first time or we're renewing it for the ump-
teenth time, we start exactly where we are now. We're either closer
to the grandson or closer to the grandfather, but wherever we are,
that's where we start.

It's said that when we make this commitment, it sows a seed
deep in our unconscious, deep in our mind and heart, that never
goes away. This seed is a catalyst that jump-starts our inherent capacity for love and compassion, for empathy, for seeing the sameness of us all. So we make the commitment, we sow the seed, then do
our best never to harden our heart or close our mind to anyone.

It's not easy to keep this vow, of course. But every time we break
it, what's important is that we recognize that we've closed someone
out, that we've distanced ourselves from someone, that we've turned
someone into the Other, the one on the opposite side of the fence.
Often we're so full of righteous indignation, so charged up, that we
don't even see that we've been triggered. But if we're fortunate, we
realize what's happened—or it's pointed out to us—and we acknowledge to ourselves what we've done. Then we simply renew our
commitment to stay open to others, aspiring to start fresh.

Some people like to read or recite an inspiring verse as part of
renewing their commitment. One we could use is the verse from
Shantideva's classic work, *The Way of the Bodhisattva,* that is traditionally repeated to reaffirm the intention to benefit others:

> Just as the awakened ones of the past
> Aroused an awakened mind
> And progressively established themselves
> In the practices of the Bodhisattva,
> So I too for the benefit of beings
> Shall arouse an awakened mind
> And progressively train myself in those practices.

We repeat these words or something similar to renew our commitment; then it's a new moment and we go forward. We will stum-
ble again and start again over and over, but as long as the seed is

planted, we will always be moving in the direction of being more and more open to others, more and more compassionate and caring.

The commitment to take care of one another, the warrior commitment, is not about being perfect. It's about continuing to put virtuous input into our unconscious, continuing to sow the seeds that predispose our heart to expand without limit, that predispose us to awaken. Every time we recognize that we've broken this commitment, rather than criticize ourselves, rather than sow seeds of self-judgment and self-denigration—or seeds of righteous indignation, rage, or whatever other frustrations we take out on other people—we can sow seeds of strength, seeds of confidence, seeds of love and compassion. We're sowing seeds so that we will become more and more like that grandfather and the many other people we know—or have heard about—who seem to be happy to put their life on the line for the sake of others.

When you do feel bad about yourself for your rigid and unforgiving heart, you can take consolation from Shantideva. He says that when he took the vow to save all sentient beings, it was "clear insanity," because even though he was unaware of it at the time, he was "subject to the same afflictions" as others—he was as confused as anyone else.

Our confusion is the confusion that everyone feels. So when you think that you've blown it in every possible way, that you've broken the commitment irredeemably, Shantideva suggests that instead of becoming mired in guilt, you view it as an incentive to spend the rest of your life recognizing your habitual tendencies and doing your best not to strengthen them.

Making the warrior commitment is like being on a sinking ship and vowing to help all the other passengers get off the boat before we do. A few years ago, I saw a perfect example of this when a US Airways plane went down in the Hudson River in New York City. Shortly after the plane took off from LaGuardia Airport, birds knocked out the engines, and the pilot had no choice but to land the plane in the river. The landing was so skillful that all 155 people aboard the aircraft survived. I can still picture them standing on the wings until they were rescued by a flotilla of small boats that rushed to the scene. The story is that the pilot stayed on the plane until everyone was safely out, then searched it again twice to make sure that no one was left behind. That's the kind of role model who embodies the warrior commitment.

On the other hand, I've also heard stories from people who were in similar situations but fled for safety without giving a thought to anyone else. They always talk about how bad that makes them feel in retrospect. One woman told me about being in a plane crash many years ago. The passengers were ordered to evacuate right away because the plane would probably blow up. The woman raced for the exit, not stopping to help anyone, not even an old man struggling to undo his seatbelt and unable to get free. Afterward, it weighed pretty heavily on her that she hadn't stopped to help him, and it has inspired her to reach out to others as much as she can, whenever she has the chance.

Shantideva says that the only way to break this vow completely is to give up altogether on wanting to help others, not caring if we're harming them because we only want to make sure that Number One is safe and secure. We run into trouble only when we close down and couldn't care less—when we're too cynical or depressed or full of doubt even to bother.

At the heart of making this commitment is training in not fearing fundamental edginess, fundamental uneasiness, when it arises in us. Our challenge is to train in smiling at groundlessness, smiling at fear. I've had years of training in this because I get panic attacks. As anyone who has experienced a panic attack knows, that feeling of terror can arise out of nowhere. For me it often comes in the middle of the night, when I'm especially vulnerable. But over the years I've trained myself to relax into that heart-stopping, mind-stopping feeling. My first reaction is always to gasp with fright. But my teacher, Chögyam Trungpa, used to gasp like that when he was describing how to recognize awakened mind. So now, whenever a panic attack comes and I gasp, I picture Chögyam Trungpa's face and think of him gasping as he talked about awakened mind. Then the energy of panic passes through me.

If you resist that kind of panicky energy, even at an involuntary, unconscious level, the fear can last a long time. The way to work with it is to drop the story line and not pull back or buy into the idea, "This isn't okay," but instead to smile at the panic, smile at this dreadful, bottomless, gaping hole that's opening up in the pit of your stomach. When you can smile at fear, there's a shift: what you usually try to escape from becomes a vehicle for awakening you to your fundamental, primordial goodness, for awakening you to clear-mindedness, to a caring that holds nothing back.

The image of the warrior is of a person who can go into the worst of hells and not waver from the direct experience of cruelty and unimaginable pain. So that's our path: even in the most difficult situations, we do our best to smile at fear, to smile at our righteous indignation, our cowardliness, our avoidance of vulnerability.

Traditionally, there are three ways of entering the warrior path, three approaches to making the commitment to benefit others. The first is called entering like a monarch—like a king or a queen. This means getting our own kingdom together, then on the basis of that strength, taking care of our subjects. The analogy is, *I work on myself and get my own life together so that I can benefit others. To the degree that I'm not triggered anymore, I can stay present and not close my mind and heart.* Our motivation is to be there for other people more and more as the years go by.

Parents get good training in this. Most mothers and fathers aspire to give their children a good life—one free of aggression or meanness. But then there's the reality of how infuriating children can be. There's the reality of losing your temper and yelling, the reality of being irritable, unreasonable, immature. When we see the discrepancy between our good intentions and our actions, it motivates us to work with our minds, to work with our habitual reactions and our impatience. It motivates us to get better at knowing our triggers and refraining from acting out or repressing. We gladly work on ourselves in order to be more skillful and loving parents.

People in the caring professions also get plenty of training in entering like a monarch. Maybe you want to work with homeless teenagers because you were once one yourself. Your desire is to make a difference in even one person's life, so they can feel that someone is there for them. Then before long, you find yourself so activated by the behavior of young people that you totally lose it and can't be there for them anymore. At that point, you turn to meditation or to the first commitment to support you in being present and open to whatever presents itself, including feelings of inadequacy, incompetence, or shame.

The next way to approach the warrior commitment is with the attitude of the ferryman. We cross the river in the company of all sentient beings—we open to our true nature together. Here the analogy is, *My pain will become the stepping-stone for understanding the pain of others.* Rather than our own suffering making us more self-absorbed, it becomes the means by which we genuinely open to others' suffering.

A number of cancer survivors have told me that this attitude is what gave them the strength to go through the physical and psychological misery of chemotherapy. They couldn't eat or drink because everything hurt too much. They had sores in their mouths. They were dehydrated. They had tremendous nausea. Then they received instruction in *tonglen.* Their world got bigger and bigger as they opened to all the other people who were experiencing the same physical pain they were, as well as the loneliness, anger, and other emotional distress that goes along with it. Their pain became a stepping-stone to understanding the distress of others in the same boat.

I remember one woman telling me, "It couldn't have gotten any worse, so I had no problem breathing in and saying, 'Since the pain is here anyway, may I take it in fully and completely with the wish that nobody else will have to feel like this.' And I had no problem sending out relief." It's not as if your nausea goes away, she said. It's not as if you can suddenly eat and drink. But the practice gives meaning to your suffering. Your attitude shifts. The feeling of resistance to the pain, the feeling of utter helplessness, and the feeling of hopelessness disappear.

There's no way to make a dreadful situation pretty. But we can use the pain of it to recognize our sameness with other people. Shantideva said that since all sentient beings suffer from strong, conflicting emotions, and all sentient beings get what they don't want and can't hold on to what they do want, and all sentient beings have physical distress, why am I making such a big deal about just me? Since we're all in this together, why am I making such a big deal about myself? The attitude of the ferryman is that whatever usually drags us down and causes us to withdraw into ourselves is the stepping-stone for awakening our compassion and for contacting the vast, unbiased mind of the warrior.

The third attitude is that of the shepherd and shepherdess, whose flock always comes first. This is the grandfather with the frogs or the pilot of the sinking plane. It's the story of firemen entering a burning building or a mother risking her life to save her child. The shepherd and shepherdess automatically put others before themselves.

Almost everyone assumes that putting others first is how we're always supposed to approach the warrior commitment. And if we do anything less, we criticize ourselves. But one way of entry isn't better than another. It could be said that we evolve toward the attitude of the shepherd and shepherdess, but it's a natural evolution. The other two approaches are no less valid. The importance of this teaching is to point out that all three approaches are admirable, beautiful, to-be-applauded ways of making the warrior commitment.

In fact, most of us use all three approaches. There are probably many examples in your life of working on yourself with the aspiration to be present and useful to other people. And there are times when your sorrow has connected you with the sorrow of others, when your grief or physical pain has been a catalyst for appreciating what another person is going through. There are also times when you spontaneously put others first.

Coldheartedness and narrow-mindedness are not the kinds of habits we want to reinforce. They won't predispose us to awakening; in fact, they will keep us stuck. So we make the warrior commitment—take the vow to care for one another—then do our best to never turn our backs on anyone. And when we falter, we renew our commitment and move on, knowing that even the awakened ones of the past understood what it felt like to relapse. Otherwise, how could they have any idea about what other beings go through? Otherwise, how could they have cultivated patience and forgiveness, loving-kindness, and compassion?

Fifty-Nine Ways to Make the Teachings Real

Judy Lief

What happens on the meditation cushion is one thing, but the real challenge is bringing our spiritual practice into the rough-and-tumble of daily life, where it can really benefit ourselves and others. Buddhist teacher Judy Lief tells us about fifty-nine ancient slogans that can help us be more skillful and loving in all our relationships.

The teachings on mind training, or *lojong*, are an invaluable aid to practitioners because they show us how the wisdom and skillful means of the Mahayana can actually be put into action. They show us how to make it real.

The lojong teachings include instruction in formless meditation, in the practice of "sending and taking" (*tonglen*), and in postmeditation practice—putting our meditation into action in our daily lives. These teachings are attributed to the great tenth-century Buddhist master Atisha Dipankara and became widely known after the Tibetan teacher Geshe Chekawa arranged and summarized them in a collection of fifty-nine mind-training sayings or reminders. Often referred to simply as the Atisha slogans, these encapsulate the essence of what it means to practice the Mahayana. The Atisha slogans are a blueprint for practicing the bodhisattva path in fifty-nine easy steps.

The power of the slogans is that they break down the Mahayana ideal of loving-kindness for us. Rather than simply giving general guidelines on how to be a true practitioner, they actually spell it out in detail. They give specific guidelines both for how to approach meditation and how to awaken in daily life. It is easy to be vaguely compassionate and generally aware-ish, but when we actually look at what we are doing and how we interact with others, it is a different matter altogether. As the saying goes, the devil is in the details.

When I first encountered the practice of tonglen and the fifty-nine mind-training slogans attributed to Atisha, I was struck by their combination of down-to-earthness and profundity. I had already been taught about the importance of joining formal sitting meditation with postmeditation practice, but apart from a vague notion of trying to be more kind and aware, I was not at all sure how to go about it. These teachings gave me a way to unpack general notions such as compassion or wisdom into specific guidelines that I could apply to my life. They placed the practice of meditation, which was what had inspired me about the tradition to begin with, within a greater and more complete understanding of practice and what it means to be a practitioner.

Studying the mind-training slogans inspired me to look into my habit of dividing meditation from everyday life, regarding it as something special and apart. When I began to really take a look at that pattern I saw that it fostered a kind of leaky approach to practice. If meditation became too intense I could escape into everyday concerns; when daily life became too overwhelming I could escape into practice. There was lots of wiggle room for neurosis. Somehow it all seemed to come back to ego and its genius for co-opting everything to further its grip on power.

The scope of the Atisha fifty-nine slogans is extensive, and they can be applied to many levels of our activity. They provide guidelines for meditation, but their real focus is on relationships of all kinds: with the earth, with our fellow humans, with our colleagues, with our closest friends, with our enemies. At first glance some of them may seem like practical advice from your grandmother. Slogans such as *Don't wallow in self-pity* may seem moralistic or even simpleminded. At the other end of the spectrum, slogans such as *Examine the nature of unborn awareness* seem to be pointing beyond the ordinary to something more ultimate and perhaps even a bit obscure. Yet they are combined into one coherent system.

Altogether, the structure of the slogans is based on the two underlying themes of Mahayana Buddhism: skillful means and wisdom. If you are to travel on the path, you need both. You need to see where you are going, and you also need a way to get there. The way to get there is what is referred to as skillful means. The cultivation of wisdom is essential, but as the old Zen saying goes, "Words don't cook rice."

With slogan practice, every situation is seen as complete, as an expression of both skillful means and wisdom. That means you do not need to look elsewhere to find the dharma, since it is present in every situation. On the other hand, it also means there is nowhere to hide. Once you have a glimpse of the extent of the teachings, they haunt you wherever you go.

Generally, no matter what you do, you need to learn how to go about it. Depending on what you want to achieve, you train in different ways. If you want to practice law, you go to law school; if you want to practice a trade, you go to trade school. And if you want to become a bodhisattva, you train in the six transcendent perfections (*paramitas*) through mind training and slogan practice.

In the Mahayana, the goal is to become a bodhisattva warrior who embodies wisdom, compassion, and openness, and the way to do that is by training in generosity, discipline, patience, exertion, and meditation. These five are the methods that will get you there, the skillful means. But those skillful means need to be joined with wisdom, or the vision to lead the way, which is *prajna*, or transcendent knowledge. Together, these six perfections (paramitas) are the Mahayana recipe for success on the path.

Working with the slogans begins to chip away at attitudes that hinder our relationships, our inner understanding, and our happiness. This chipping-away process begins with meditation practice, with the pacifying of our restless mind. With that foundation, we can begin the practice of tonglen. In tonglen, we practice reversing the habit of viewing everything purely through the lens of our own self-interest. Instead we begin to appreciate how we are continually in interchange with other beings. So tonglen opens up the possibility of relating in a more flowing and genuine way, one less caught up in fear and self-protection. We see that we do not have to just passively accept the relationship patterns we have fallen into. We can make changes.

In tonglen, we breathe out what we normally cling to and breathe in what we usually avoid. In doing so, we work with qualities within ourselves and with issues that arise in relating to others. The Atisha slogan related to this is number seven: *Sending and taking should be practiced alternately. These two should ride the breath.*

It may seem crazy to practice breathing in what you do not want and breathing out what you desire, but rather than being self-destructive, this exercise is surprisingly liberating. You discover that the habit of trying to protect yourself by holding on to some things and getting rid of others does not really protect you; it just makes you mildly paranoid and defensive all the time. When you are not battling against whatever is bugging you at the moment, but really breathe it in, you realize that you don't have to take everything that happens to you as a personal attack. It is just what is happening, and you can find a way to deal with it.

On the sending-out side, you begin to realize that you do not have to parcel out your limited store of goodness or health for fear of running out, and you can let it flow more freely. The less you try to hold on to whatever virtue you have as your little treasure, the more there seems to be. Making it your possession has been like trying to drive with the parking brake engaged.

This practice is remarkable in its effects. When you are not so caught up in sucking in goodies and warding off threats, when you are not so attached to perfection and afraid of flaws, you can come to accept yourself and others in a new and fresh way. This reduces burnout and defeatism. When people encounter you, they sense that you are not trying to use them, even subtly, to further your own schemes. I think this is one reason that tonglen is such a healing force and is so helpful for people who work with pain and suffering in their line of work.

With slogan practice, we step-by-step liberate trapped energy, energy recruited to the project of propping up ego. That project is based on fear. Whenever we mess up, we worry about being caught. We even worry about catching ourselves. So we waste a lot of energy covering up, being defensive, or making excuses.

According to slogan twelve—*Drive all blames into one*—most of our problems can be traced to one underlying cause: ego fixation. Until we start to deal with this level, we will only be treating symptoms. With this slogan we take responsibility for our own actions. Instead of hiding our mistakes, we face them and look for their underlying cause. And the more we look, the more we understand the power of ego-clinging and the damage it does. We begin to have a glimpse of what a difference it makes when we are not carrying around the hidden agenda of ego.

This slogan is also helpful when we are dealing with groups, where it is common to get in struggles about who is to blame, as though finding the guilty party will solve the problem. With this slogan you take on the blame yourself, no matter what the case. By doing so, the process can shift from one of finger-pointing to one of problem solving, to the benefit of the whole organization. This does not mean that you do not try to discover where specific problems arise. In fact you are more apt to figure this out, since you have removed the need for others to cover up or to defend themselves from attack.

Another powerful lesson of slogan practice is how to relate to the ups and downs of life. Slogan forty-two—*Whichever of the two occurs, be patient*—is a reminder of how easily we are swept away by the excitement of things going our way or the disappointment of things not working out for us. When things are going well, we forget that it will inevitably change. Witness the optimism of the housing bubble. When things go downhill, we tend to get in a funk and see no way out. Witness the doomsday phenomenon.

This fluctuation in circumstances can take place on a grand scale or simply as the ups and downs of an ordinary day. Instead of just experiencing what we are experiencing, we either hope to get out of it or fear losing it. The practice of this slogan is to stay with present experience and not assume anything about what may follow. This allows us to find our ground in ever-shifting circumstances, and by example to provide that ground for others.

The Atisha slogans conclude with number fifty-nine: *Don't expect applause.* When we are always looking over our shoulder to see how others think we are doing, it is hard to act directly and skillfully. The result of our need for recognition is that we feel disheartened, belittled, or furious when it does not materialize. It is hard to maintain steady effort when we give that power over to others, and we find that we are not really in tune with what we are doing. With this slogan, instead of looking for recognition from outside, we develop the confidence to trust the action itself for feedback. If outside recognition comes, that's great, but if not, it's no big deal.

The mind-training slogans skillfully prod us to lighten up and drop our pretentiousness. Instead of just talking about being loving or compassionate, they spell out how to do it. Their focus is on actions, not just attitude. We could have all sorts of loving and kind thoughts, and feel all warm and fuzzy, but so what? The point is to help this world, ourselves, and others at the same time, and we have the means to do so. Every time we are pricked awake by one of the slogans, and adjust our attitude or behavior, we expand our understanding of what it is to be skillful.

Working with the Atisha slogans is a wonderful way to bring practice into all aspects of your life. They work not by grand gestures, but by the accumulation of many little interruptions to the momentum of ego confusion. In the midst of activity, a slogan pops up, and in an instant you change course. In that way, little by little, ordinary actions are liberated into bodhisattva activity. Because it is so easy to lose track of practice mentality and work from a more shallow and conventional fallback position, it is good that we have these handy reminders to wake us up on the spot. Through the power of mind training, we never run out of opportunities to flip our limited actions into the skillful methodology of the bodhisattva path, and our limited vision into the penetrating insight of prajna.

Contemplating the Slogans

Choose one of the following lojong slogans to work with over a period of three days: *Be grateful to everyone; Always maintain only a joyful mind; Don't try to be fastest; Don't be swayed by external circumstances;* or *Always meditate on whatever provokes resentment.*

On the first day, use the slogan to reflect on how you relate to your spiritual practice.

On the second day, bring the slogan to mind in reflecting on how you handle personal relationships.

On the third day, apply the slogan to your relationships with colleagues and your approach to your work.

Open Heart, Open Mind

Tsoknyi Rinpoche

According to Vajrayana Buddhism, the fast track to awakening is to look directly at your own mind and discover its true nature. Tsoknyi Rinpoche shows us how we can experience two profound qualities—emptiness and clarity—of enlightened mind. Our mind.

As a young child I used to sit on my grandfather's lap while he meditated. At two or three years old, of course, I had no idea what meditation involved. My grandfather didn't give me instructions and didn't speak to me about his own experience. Yet, as I sat with him I felt a sense of deep comfort, together with a kind of childlike fascination with whatever was going on around me. I felt myself becoming aware of something becoming brighter and more intense in my own body, my own mind, my own heart.

That something, when I was old enough to fit words to it, is a kind of spark that lights the lives of all living beings. It has been given various names by people of many different disciplines, and its nature has been debated for centuries.

In many Buddhist teachings, it's known as "buddhanature." The term is a very rough translation of two Sanskrit words, often used interchangeably: *sugatagarbha* or *tathagatagarbha*. *Sugata* may be roughly understood as "gone to bliss," while *thatagata* is usually interpreted as "thus-gone." Both refer to those, like the Buddha, who have transcended, or "gone beyond," conflict, delusion, or suffering of any kind—a condition one might reasonably understand as "blissful." *Garbha* is most commonly translated as "essence," although on a subtle level, it may also suggest "seed" or "root." So a more accurate translation of "buddhanature" might be the essence of one who has gone beyond conflict, delusion, and so on to an experience of unclouded bliss. One of the core teachings of Buddhism is that we all possess this essence, this root or seed.

Buddhanature is hard to describe, largely because it is limitless. It's a bit difficult to contain the limitless within the sharp boundaries of words and images. Although the actual experience of touching our awakened nature defies absolute description, a number of people over the past two millennia have at least tried to illuminate a course of action using words that serve as lights along the way.

EMPTINESS

Traditionally, one of the words that describes the basis of who and what we are—indeed, the basis of all phenomena—has been translated as "emptiness"; a word that, at first glance, might seem a little scary, a suggestion, supported by early translators and interpreters of Buddhist philosophy, that there is some sort of void at the center of our being.

Most of us, at some point in our lives, have experienced some sort of emptiness. We've wondered, "What am I doing here?" "Here" may be a job, a relationship, a home, a body with creaking joints, a mind with fading memories.

If we look deeper, though, we can see that the void we may experience in our lives is actually a positive prospect.

"Emptiness" is a rough translation of the Sanskrit term *shunyata* and the Tibetan term *tongpa-nyi*. The basic meaning of the Sanskrit word *shunya* is "zero," while the Tibetan word *tongpa* means "empty"—not in the sense of a vacuum or a void, but rather in the sense that the basis of experience is beyond our ability to perceive with our senses and or to capture in a nice, tidy concept. Maybe a better understanding of the deep sense of the word may be "inconceivable" or "unnameable."

So when Buddhists talk about emptiness as the basis of our being, we don't mean that who or what we are is nothing, a zero, a point of view that can give way to a kind of cynicism. The actual teachings on emptiness imply an infinitely open space that allows for anything to appear, change, disappear, and reappear. The basic meaning of emptiness, in other words, is openness, or potential. At the basic level of our being, we are "empty" of definable characteristics. We aren't defined by our past, our present, or our thoughts and feelings about the future. We have the potential to experience anything. And "anything" can refer to thoughts, feelings, and physical sensations.

AN EMPTINESS EXERCISE

I'd like to give you a little taste of emptiness through a practice that has become known as "objectless *shinay*." *Shinay* is a Tibetan term, a combination of two words: *shi*—which is commonly translated as "calmness" or "peace"—and *nay*, which means "resting," or simply "staying there." In Sanskrit, this practice is known as *shamatha*. Like *shi*, *shama* may be understood in a variety of ways, including "peace," "rest," or "cooling down," while *tha*, like *nay*, means to "abide" or "stay." Whether in Sanskrit or Tibetan, the combination terms describe a process of cooling down from a state of mental, emotional, or sensory excitement.

Most of us, when we look at something, hear something, or experience a thought or motion, react almost automatically with some sort of judgment. This judgment can fall into three basic categories: pleasant ("I like this"), unpleasant ("I don't like this"), or confused ("I don't know whether I like this or not"). Each of these categories is often subdivided into smaller categories: pleasant experiences are judged as "good," for example; unpleasant experiences are judged as "bad." As far as one student expressed it, the confused judgment is just too puzzling: "I usually try to push it out of my mind and focus on something else." The possibilities represented by all these different responses, however, tempt us to latch on to our judgments and the patterns that underlie them, undermining our attempt to distinguish between real and true.

There are many varieties of shamatha practice. The one that most closely approaches an experiential rather than a theoretical understanding of emptiness is known commonly as "objectless," because it doesn't involve—as some other variations do—focusing attention on a particular object, like a sound, or a smell, or a physical thing like a flower, a crystal, or a candle flame.

The instructions for this meditation are simple:

- Just straighten your spine while keeping the rest of your body relaxed.
- Take a couple of deep breaths.
- Keep your eyes open, though not so intently that your eyes begin to burn or water. You can blink. But just notice yourself blinking. Each blink is an experience of nowness.
- Now, let yourself be aware of everything you're experiencing— sights, sounds, physical sensations, thoughts, and emotions.
- Allow yourself to be open to all these experiences.

Inevitably, as you begin this exercise, all sorts of thoughts, feelings, and sensations will pass through your experience. This is to be expected. This little exercise is in many ways like starting a weight-training program at the gym. At first you can lift only a few pounds for a few repetitions before your muscles get tired. But if you keep at it, gradually you'll find that you can lift heavier weights and perform more repetitions.

Similarly, learning to connect with nowness is a gradual process. At first you might be able to remain open for only a few seconds at a time before thoughts, emotions, and sensations bubble up to the surface and consume your attention. The basic instruction is simply not to chase after these but merely to be aware of everything that passes through your awareness as it is. Whatever you experience, you don't have to suppress it. Even latching onto irritations—"Oh, I wish that kid next door could turn down his music"; "I wish the family upstairs would stop yelling at each other"—are part of the present. Just observe these thoughts and feelings come and go—and how quickly they come and go, to be replaced by others. If you keep doing this, you'll get a true taste of emptiness—a vast, open space in which possibilities emerge and combine, dance together for a while, and vanish with astonishing rapidity. You've tasted one aspect of your basic nature, which is the freedom to experience anything and everything.

Don't criticize or condemn yourself if you find yourself following after physical sensations, thoughts, or emotions. No one becomes a buddha overnight. Recognize, instead, that for a few seconds you were directly able to experience something new, something now. You've passed through theory and ventured into the realm of experience. As we begin to let our experiences come and go, we begin to see them as less solid. They may be real, but we begin to question whether they're true.

Experience follows intention. Wherever we are, whatever we do, all we need to do is recognize our thoughts, feelings, and perceptions as something natural. Neither rejecting nor accepting, we simply acknowledge the experience and let it pass. If we keep this up, we'll eventually find ourselves becoming able to manage situations we once found painful, scary, or sad. We'll discover a sense of confidence that isn't rooted in arrogance or pride. We'll realize that we're always sheltered, always safe, and always home.

CLARITY

The exercise described above raises another aspect of our basic nature, and now I'm going to let you in on a little bit of unconventional understanding.

As mentioned earlier, according to many standard Tibetan

translations, the syllable *nyi* means "ness"—the essential quality of a thing. But I was taught that the *nyi* of *tongpa-nyi*, on a symbolic level, refers to clarity: the capacity to be aware of all the things we experience, to see the stuff of our experience and to know that we're seeing it.

This capacity is the cognizant aspect of our nature: a very simple, basic capability for awareness. This basic, or natural, awareness is merely a potential. Just as emptiness is a capacity to be anything, clarity is the capacity to see anything that enables us to recognize and distinguish the unlimited variety of thoughts, feelings, sensations, and appearances that continually emerge out of emptiness. Without clarity, we wouldn't be able to recognize or identify any aspect of our experience. It's not connected with awareness of any particular thing. Awareness of a thing—in terms of a subject (the one who is aware) and an object (the thing, experience, etc., of which the subject is aware)—is something we learn as we grow up.

This cognizant, or knowing, aspect of our nature is often described in Tibetan as *ö-sel-wa*, which can also be translated as "luminosity"—a fundamental capacity to illuminate, or shed light on, our experiences and, thus, to know or be aware of them. In his teachings, the Buddha sometimes compared it to a house in which a lamp has been lit and the shades or shutters have been drawn. The house represents the patterns that bind us to a seemingly solid perspective of ourselves and the world around us. The lamp represents our luminous quality of the spark of our basic nature. No matter how tightly the shades and shutters are closed, inevitably a bit of the light from inside the house shines through. Inside the house, the light from the lamp provides the clarity to distinguish between, say, a chair, a bed, or a carpet—which corresponds to our personal thoughts, feelings, and physical sensations. As this light seeps through the shades or shutters we see other things—people, places, or events. Such experiences may be dualistic; that is to say, a tendency to perceive our experience in terms of self and other, "me" and "not me," but if we take a moment even to appreciate such glimpses we can arrive at a deeper, broader experience of basic, or natural, clarity.

Meditation: Tasting Clarity

To experience clarity it is often necessary to embark on another sha-matha exercise, this time using a formal object as the focus of our attention. I advise using a physical object like a clear glass, because that object is already clear and transparent. Start off by setting such an object where it can easily be seen whether you're sitting in a chair, on a meditation cushion, or on the floor.

Take a few moments to rest in objectless shamatha in order to open yourself to experience. Then look at the object you've cho-sen—no longer than a minute for a little while—a process that isn't all that different from staring at a TV screen or a person ahead of us in a line at a grocery store.

Then, slowly, slowly, turn your attention from the object of at-tention to the aspect of your being that is capable of perceiving ob-jects. Recognize your ability to simply see and experience things. This ability is all too often taken for granted.

When we first begin to rest our attention on an object, we tend to see it as distinct or separate from ourselves. The capacity to make such distinctions is, according to neuroscientists and psychologists with whom I've spoken, in part a survival mechanism that helps us distinguish between objects in our environment that can harm us and objects that can help us. This survival mechanism, in turn, in-fluences our internal sense of "I" as uniquely defined beings—solid and separate from "not I."

Now, let's just take a taste of clarity:

- First, just rest in open presence.
- Then turn your attention to the object on which you've cho-sen to focus.

Thoughts, feelings, and judgments about the object will almost inevitably arise: "This is pretty." "This is ugly." "This is—I don't know—it's just a glass." You may even wonder, as I did many years ago when I was first taught this practice, "Why am I doing this?"

The point of the practice—the "why" of it—lies in the next step:

- After focusing for a few moments on an object, turn your attention inward, from the object to the awareness that perceives not only the object, but also the various thoughts, feelings, judgments surrounding it.

As you do so, a very gentle experience of what many of my teachers called "awareness of being aware" emerges. You'll begin to recognize that whatever you see, however you see it, is accompanied by emotional and cognitive residue—the stuff that remains from being a neglected child, a failure in the eyes of parents or teachers, the victim of a schoolyard bully.

When we turn our awareness inward, we begin to decompress the images we hold about ourselves and the world around us. In so doing, we begin to use the process of distinction rather than be used by it. We begin to see how past experiences might turn into present patterns. We glimpse the possibility of a connection between what we see and our capacity to see.

Waking Up to Happiness

Natalie Goldberg

Sneezing, coughing, blowing her nose—Natalie Goldberg is awfully sick.
And yet she is happy. On her sickbed, she realizes that happiness is
available all the time, but we can only find it when we're still.

Last summer I was sick in bed. I could write "flu" and be done with
it, but that would be a generalization. My eyes were blood-red and
caked shut in the morning—the doctor said it was conjunctivitis.
"Isn't that what little kids get?" I asked. A lump was developing in
the bottom of my mouth. I coughed up green phlegm. My ears were
ringing and I heard things as though I were underwater.

Why do I feel the need to state all this? While sick, I read *The
Makioka Sisters*, by Junichiro Tanizaki. The book was long, slow,
magnificent, and included everything—many details about the
main characters' colds, allergies, bug bites, and intestinal problems.
But as I read, I didn't cringe or back away. We are in human bodies
and sickness is natural, a part of this physical life.

I took extra delight in the book's last line. The third sister was
finally going to be married—one of the strong narrative drives
throughout the book—and the result: "Yukiko's diarrhea persisted
through the twenty-sixth, and was a problem on the train to Tokyo."

And so the book ends. We are left with the ginger hesitation of a woman in her thirties—late for marriage in mid-twentieth-century Japan—riding to her destiny, her body engaged and nervously pumping. Now don't be a prude. You have to love it. The honesty alone. No one else tells us these things. Thank the writer for being honest.

While I was sick, lying in bed reading, I'd occasionally look up through my bedroom window and watch the pale green on the distant willows and near lilacs. And sometimes I'd pause to sneeze, cough, blow my nose, take a sip of tea. Friends would call to commiserate. Yes, I was awfully sick—it did seem a long time to be in bed—then I'd return to the dream of the book in hand.

The truth is I was happy. Happier than I'd been in a long, long time. Yet I knew that as soon as my energy returned I'd plunge back into mad activity, full of passion. I was lucky because I loved most of what I did in life, but as I lay in bed I realized passion was different than happiness. You don't *do* happiness. You receive it. It's like a water table under the earth. It's available to everyone but we can only tap it, have it run up through us, when we're still. A well that darts around can never draw water.

We misinterpret success, desire, enterprise, and the things we love as the state of happiness. Usually, we don't even consider happiness because we're too busy dashing after life, defending, building, developing, even fighting, asserting, arguing. We're in the scramble—lively, engaged. So where does happiness come in? It's a give and take, a meeting of inside and outside. Even enlightenment is a meeting, a relationship of the inside and outside. The Buddha was enlightened—his whole nervous system switched gears—when he glanced up and saw the morning star. We don't wake up in a vacuum. We can't be at home with ourselves in a cubicle. To be at home with ourselves is to be at home in the world, in the interaction with others—and trees and slices of cheese and the broad, sad evolving of politics.

When I was sick, I was settled down. I didn't have a lot of energy for engagement, the daily tending to a hundred details. I am not saying the ideal state is a sick body, but when I began to aggravate about something I knew I was getting better. When the bite of concern and worry snapped in, I was reentering the pale of human life. At that moment, where was my happiness? I lost my connection to home plate, to the core of reception, patience, the bottom of my belly, to the ground of well-being.

The next day I dragged myself out of bed and crossed my legs, sitting up straight for half an hour to anchor my wandering mind in the breath. To keep coming back to the present moment. To regain the contentment I'd so quickly lost.

As I sat, I was lost for a long time in a memory of Auschwitz, where I'd meditated for five days the previous summer, then I was lost in the thought of turning over the compost out back in my yard, then in considering maybe buying some granola. Thoughts have no hierarchy. The mind jumps from the serious to the mundane in a second. Then snap. I came back to myself. If I want happiness I have to understand it and then dedicate myself to it moment by moment. I can't stay in bed sick all the time to attain it. I have to commit myself to it when I'm also well.

The thing I love about the Zen koans, those terse, enigmatic teachings from the Chinese ancestors, is that they include sickness in their presentations to realize original nature.

Great Master Ma was not well. The director of the monastery stopped in his room and inquired, "How is your health? How are you feeling?" The Great Master replied, "Sun Face Buddha, Moon Face Buddha."

We could speculate on meaning here, but the important thing right now is that sickness is included in the realm of realizing peace, understanding, and happiness. Nothing left out. How can we stay connected to contentment in the dentist's chair? How can we be with peace as we listen to the news? Sometimes happiness is being in the center of our grief.

When my friend's husband died in his thirties and she was bereft, her therapist said, "Enjoy your grief. You'll miss it when it's gone." Can you imagine that? To be in the heart of your life whatever your heart holds.

I am not saying there is a prescription for happiness. Just that the trained mind examines situations; it does not simply fall apart. If you are sick in bed, it's an opportunity. If you continually have a hard time with a friend, look deeper than the bickering and misunderstandings. Maybe the relationship died years ago and you neglected to notice it, hanging on to old ideas of love. Maybe it will take root again—maybe not.

In college, the single class that caught my interest was an ethics class in the philosophy department. We studied Descartes, Bergson, James, Kant, Socrates, the full gamut of white dead Western men. The essence of each reading was the question of happiness. What is it? How to attain it?

When I studied with my Japanese Zen teacher he said, "Whatever you do, let it be accompanied by dharma joy." He lifted his dark eyebrows in an expression of inclusion. Yes, you, too, Natalie, are capable of this. At the time I was thirty-one years old.

No one can hand over happiness on a silver plate—or on a doily. Especially when we don't know what it is. Our job is to pay attention and examine it. Can we have happiness and peace at the same time as joy, fun, pleasure, anger, and aggression? How do we learn to abide in ourselves?

I ended up staying sick in bed for five weeks. That's a long time. My ears, the eustachian tubes, became congested. The middle of my head filled up. Finally, on a Wednesday, I had some energy and went out. Eagerly I plunged into life again. How foolish I was. I must have done thirty different tasks, including going out that night with friends. I enjoyed it all, but just as I was falling asleep, I asked myself the question, "Were you happy?" Quickly the answer came: only the half hour I was planting tomatoes and strawberries in the backyard.

The next morning I woke with the black stranger loneliness sitting beside me. Certainly I've been lonely before, but this time it manifested heavily beside me. I'd lost paradise, my time in bed.

In the next days at different intervals I asked myself, "Are you happy?" Head deep in my active life, I didn't know how to find happiness again. I couldn't make it happen. Then just seven days out of bed, standing in line at the bank, like a cocker spaniel or possum, I felt happiness, for absolutely no reason, ringing my bell. After I made my deposit, I sat in the car wondering what had happened. I was almost "bursting with happiness," as they say in romance novels, but I was not particularly in love, only swimming in my own being.

Then this morning, as I dressed to go out, I again asked myself, "Are you happy?" I was darkly blue from allergies and constant May winds and a drought that made my skin almost crackle, so I growled "no" but I wasn't convincing. Some defense had been smashed. Even in misery there could be happiness. And then it bubbled up, clear and full, for no reason. But there *was* a reason. I was paying attention.

Happiness is shy. It wants to know you want it. You can't be greedy. You can't be numb—or ignorant. The bashful girl of happiness needs your kind attention. Then she'll come forward. And you won't have to be sick to find her.

The Long Road to Sitting Still

Pico Iyer

Wherever you go, according to the old saying, there you are. It's deeper than it sounds. Wherever you go, you bring the baggage of your ego and neuroses with you. And whenever you go, the reality of your enlightened nature is always there too. In fact, Buddhists have long recommended leaving home as a good way to shed our temporary identities and touch deeper truths. One of the great modern exponents of travel as contemplative practice is the best-selling writer Pico Iyer.

"There is no Garden of Eden" was the judgment that greeted me, as an impressionable boy, in the pages of my teenage hero, D. H. Lawrence, "and the Hesperides never were." Lawrence was my hero, though, precisely because he could never stay fixed in any one dogma and was intensely alive to the limitations of his own perspective. So he continued, "Yet, in our very search for them, we touch the coasts of illusion and come into contact with other worlds." Touching the coasts of illusion was not something I was wild about at fifteen—and no one has yet described the incandescent English novelist as a Buddhist—but in his restless movements both within and without, Lawrence seemed to be offering a useful challenge (and complement) to the injunction I see whenever I step into a temple in Kyoto, aimed at innocent seekers after truth: "Look Beneath Your Feet."

A Buddhist, at least in theory, is more aware than most that travel, as Emerson had it, is a fool's paradise if you think you can find anything abroad that you couldn't find at home; everything we need is here and now. The Buddha himself found all the reality he required just sitting in one place. And to travel in search of anything is an even greater invitation to illusion, if only because expectation so reliably defeats itself. In the classic Sufi story, a holy fool who has lost his key in his living room circles around in the street, looking for it there. Why? Because there's more light in the street, he says, underneath the lamps.

And yet, and yet: not many months ago, I went up to a little fishing village in northern Japan with the Dalai Lama. The place had been leveled during the tsunami eight months earlier—thousands had been washed away to sea—and, as soon as he heard about the tragedy on the BBC, the Dalai Lama told the villagers, he knew he had to come to visit the people who remained there. There was little he could do, practically speaking, to help those who had lost almost everything, but he could at least remind them that they were not alone.

Over and over, during the week I spent with him on his annual November trip to Japan, he used the word "pilgrimage" of his trip to Tohoku. A "pilgrimage," he might have been saying, is a journey into reality, the facts of old age, suffering, and death that we are obliged to observe and then to work with; a pilgrimage is a journey into others, too, the necessary complement to the four hours of meditation the Tibetan lama observes every morning alone. A pilgrimage is a journey into community and the world and what we can possibly share with others. "Going out," as John Muir famously had it, is "really going in."

Sitting in the little temple that had somehow withstood the oncoming water, the boxed remains of those who had no relatives to claim them at his side, the lifelong pilgrim in red robes recalled how he knew a little of what his listeners were going through because he, too, in 1959, had suddenly been forced to leave his home, without even saying good-bye to his friends "and one small dog." A few days later, even as he drew closer to freedom, he heard that many of those he'd left behind had been killed.

Nearly all my travels, I sometimes feel, have been an attempt to journey deeper into the wisdom of my favorite traveler—and Emerson's friend—Henry David Thoreau: "It is not worth the while to go round the world to count the cats in Zanzibar." Thoreau is thought to have translated excerpts from the *Lotus Sutra* into English (from French) a few years before he wrote those words, and given us all a bracing example of how real exploration and truth come from sitting in one place, seeing through—in every sense of those words—all the delusions and projections we foist upon the world, especially when we assume that real life or understanding is happening somewhere else. He found India, China, Persia in Walden Pond; he found life and death and friendship and solitude.

"I measure distance inward," he pointed out, and "to travel and 'descry new lands' is to think new thoughts and have new imaginings." And yet these new imaginings and thoughts sometimes come to us most powerfully when we're surrounded by the alien, or what we cannot understand, and the very act of taking off on a journey speaks for a kind of openness and ripeness that is in fact the first step on the road to transformation. It's a public recognition that you don't know everything and that some of those things can come to you as readily on the road as on the mat; it's a way of setting your senses at the level marked "ON," slapping yourself awake and trying to join that much larger sense of self—or non-self—we sometimes lose when we're sleepwalking through our lives.

And so I take myself off, often to pilgrimage spots sacred to other people—Jerusalem, Varanasi, Koyasan, the rich red interior of Australia—in order to witness the truths of the billions outside myself. Go to the Jokhang Temple at the center of Lhasa and, in its flickering candlelight, see the excited faces, the tears, the deeply human hopes that people are bringing to its statues, many of them having traveled thousands of miles to be there, some having prostrated every step of the way. See the Dalai Lama himself, born to a very isolated land, visibly savoring the opportunity to travel and learn from other traditions, while refining and deepening his clear and objective sense of what the world is. Like the man he calls his "boss," the Buddha, this doctor of the mind realizes that the first mandate of any physician is, as it were, to take the temperature and assess the condition of his patient, whether that's himself or someone sitting outside himself; he also reminds us that the first mandate of any patient is to go out and see the doctor—who is not always, or unfailingly, himself.

From Basho to Thich Nhat Hanh, Buddhists have traveled, precisely to remind themselves of the importance of alertness ("Develop a mind that alights nowhere," as the *Lotus Sutra* says), even if they never forget that the core of their practice is stillness. Physical movement is not in itself important, but it can be the catalyst, as Lawrence pointed out, to being moved or taken out of yourself; one of the easiest ways of jolting oneself awake and free of habits and assumptions. Look outside your window; walk outside your room. Drive across town to where three Vietnamese in their restaurant are bringing almost unimaginable stories of suffering and persistence to the town in which you were born.

Why go round the world to count the cats in Zanzibar, I tell my beloved teacher Thoreau? Because you have something to give those cats, beyond just counting them. Because counting them is how you can get them placed on an "endangered species" list and make sure they have a future. Because counting the cats in Zanzibar is a way of putting Santa Cruz in perspective. Because the fellow travelers you meet along the road to Zanzibar may have so much in common with you that you can learn from them, and give to them, as you could not so easily do at home.

One of the great pilgrimage stories in any tradition, surely, is *The Snow Leopard*, by Peter Matthiessen. At the very dawn of his Zen studies, Matthiessen goes, with a professional zoologist, to count the cats in Inner Dolpo in Nepal and to set eyes on one of the world's rare and elusive creatures. But he's also traveling, we soon realize, to see through the folly of such a venture (for him, not a professional zoologist). He's traveling to look past the delusions of travel, to come face to face with the world and the memory of the young wife he's just lost to cancer, so easily sidestepped if he were to stay at home. He's traveling to see how the Buddhism that he's beginning to learn about instructs and guides those born to the tradition; he's traveling into isolation and high altitudes to confront his own anger and restlessness and spiritual ambition,

He didn't see the snow leopard, which makes the whole trip worthwhile.

It's not pilgrimage, in other words, that's our undoing; it's the thought that we will get anything out of it. Become a pilgrim with no agenda—no hope of finding anything—and who knows what may come to you? The problem is rarely in the activity, but in the hopes that we bring to it; everything can be a pilgrimage—even a trip to a tsunami-stricken fishing village—if only you can approach it in the right spirit, with clear-eyed attention.

There is humility in the act of pilgrimage, akin to the act of bowing; you're surrendering your own path to follow where others have gone before. It puts you in place, in that sense, and your intentions in perspective. There's community, of course, because you're journeying with all those others, across centuries and continents, who have also traveled to Bodh Gaya or Sarnath, and as much as anything, you're walking in their footsteps and in their shoes. There's truthfulness in the act, if it can get you out of your head, the place where you end up when sitting still lacks discipline or direction. There's kindness, if the cats of Zanzibar need something you can give them, even if it's only (as with the snow leopard) the wisdom to leave them alone.

On his same trip to Japan last November, the Dalai Lama made a pilgrimage to Koyasan, the mountain sacred to practitioners in the Shingon sect of Buddhism and one of the country's central pilgrim-

age sites. At the top of the mountain in the center of the central island, not far from Osaka, he arrived at a place that has little other
than 200,000 graves, groves of giant cedar trees that have been there
for 800 years, and 117 Shingon temples, sustaining a meditative tradition that goes back to Kobo Daishi, who founded the first temple
on the mountain 1,200 years ago.

Sleeping on tatami mats and eating Japanese vegetarian food
three times a day was not always easy for the Tibetans who were
traveling with His Holiness. But one of them, a high lama himself,
told me that, for all the discomforts—maybe because of them—he
was able to meditate with a clarity and intensity not easy to find
anywhere in the world. As if by contagion, and drawing on the energy of the hundreds of monks all around, the *yamabushi* (or mountain ascetics) with their strange shamanic outfits among the trees,
the busloads of pilgrims all in white who had passed through 88
temples on the island of Shikoku to come to this great climax of
their journeying, he could plug himself into something larger than
himself, and new to him.

I came back home after spending a week with the Tibetans and
reflected on how there are pilgrims in almost every tradition, but
Siddhartha Gautama, the Dalai Lama's "boss," was one of those who
had most stressed (in his example and his words) the necessity of
leaving one's gilded palace behind in order to meet what's real and
see how the other half (which is to say, every sentient being but
yourself) lives. He'd even had to leave the people he loved and the
life he knew—like the Dalai Lama in 1959—in order to be of service
to them. When the Dalai Lama used the word "pilgrim," he—as
ever—wasn't being casual. The Buddha himself, of course, traveled
for six years to see through the lures of austerity as much as of
indulgence and to learn what teachers couldn't offer him and what
he could locate only in himself. He slept in graveyards and on beds
of thorns; he ate only a single grain of rice at times and sometimes,
it's said, held his breath until he almost expired.

That act of directed journeying was part of what has moved
people from every tradition—whether their names are Somerset

Maugham or Hermann Hesse or, in fact, D. H. Lawrence—to take him as an inspiration and as a fellow traveler who was responding to some intuition that said that what he saw in his enclosure wasn't everything. I remember how, when I left my own enchanted garden in a tiny way at the age of twenty-nine, quitting my apartment on Park Avenue South and my twenty-fifth-floor office in Rockefeller Center to go and live in a monastery in Kyoto, I took heart from the Buddha's precedent and felt that a wise man had walked this path before me, aware that there must be something more in a life than just external rewards and a child's notion of success.

Of course the monastery couldn't be the place I'd romantically fashioned in my head, but I had to go there to find that out and, in the finding, to realize that simple alternatives to worldliness were likely to be as much a dead end as a résumé unless they were accompanied by a wide-awake eye and a spirit of discernment. The Buddha found what he had to see by sitting still, but even he had to travel to get to that point, to see through the other roads that would lead nowhere and, with Peter Matthiessen, come finally to the understanding that the truth we're looking for is no further than the hair on our arms.

Christians and Muslims observe great and classic pilgrimages, and so do people set on their own course, but the Buddha, perhaps, taking the Middle Way and always reminding us that even our destination is unfixed and perhaps illusory, is every walker's special friend. Those who journey with him know that they may not come to knowledge so much as a deepened sense of their own ignorance. Even after he arrived at the Bodhi tree, Siddhartha had to sit through night after night before finally waking up to the truth he'd been carrying with him every moment.

And then, of course, he took to the road again, for the next forty-five years, across the plains and cities of the central Gangetic plain, if only to tell people to become lamps unto themselves. His very last words seem to suggest that the journey is perpetual: "All created things move on. Keep striving with diligence."

"In one sense we are always traveling," Thomas Merton wrote, "traveling as if we did not know where we are going. In another sense we have already arrived." The lives of each of us, the Buddha was saying on his path, are a journey toward recognizing where we've been all along.

Emotional Chaos to Clarity

Phillip Moffitt

*One of our biggest problems in life is what Buddhism calls "conflicting
emotions." Anger, jealousy, greed, lust, and so forth—these are the chaotic
emotions and impulsive actions that conflict with reality, cause conflict
within us, and create all kinds of conflict with others. Fortunately, as
Phillip Moffitt tells us, Buddhist practice offers effective techniques to
calm conflicting emotions and transform their chaos into clarity.*

If you are motivated to bring more clarity to the chaos of your
mind, it is crucial that you have some kind of practice for staying
present and aware during its moment-to-moment movement.
Mindfulness meditation, the practice I teach, comes from the Theravada Buddhist tradition of *vipassana*, or "insight," meditation. The
practice of mindfulness meditation trains you to be present and
aware in daily life. When you are being mindful, you are better able
to see clearly what is happening in each moment of your life. As a
result you gain new insights into your experience, which greatly
enhances your ability to tolerate difficult situations and to make
wiser decisions.

In mindfulness practice you *practice being an observer of your experience, in the moment, as you are having it.* You begin noticing how your body responds to whatever is happening. For instance, you develop the habit of noticing stress is manifesting in your body in the form of raised shoulders, tight jaw, or neck muscles, or stirrings in the belly. You start with awareness of the body because it is easy to know and brings you into the present moment. It also grounds your emotions and stops you from getting lost in your thoughts.

Once you have developed the ability to be present with what you are experiencing in your body, you start to pay attention to the other dimensions of your experience. You learn to notice whether what is happening in your body feels pleasant or unpleasant or neutral, and you observe how that feeling affects your thoughts and words. As you become skilled at being aware of bodily sensations, you then start to observe that every emotion and every mind state has a pleasant, unpleasant, or neutral quality, which helps you develop the habit of noticing your mind states and emotions in any given moment. For instance, you may repeatedly experience frustration, irritation, or anxiety by the end of your work day.

Through mindfulness you begin to notice the early warning signs in your body of unpleasant emotions and mind states arising. And you discover that they are not you but rather the result of impersonal causes and conditions—work overload, a difficult boss or coworker, deadline pressures, and so forth—exacerbated by your mind's reaction to the unpleasantness and uncertainty. You then realize that you can choose not to fall into anxiety or irritation and can instead relax your body, interrupt the unskillful mind pattern, and reframe how you view your situation. Even though unpleasant moments still occur, your work life has gained a new ease and clarity. The difference is that you no longer identify with your emotions and mind states or allow them to determine the nature of your experience.

During the mindfulness process, you do not judge, compare, or try to fix your emotions or mind states. Instead you learn to be fully present to whatever you are experiencing, with a calm, nonjudgmental mind and an open heart. Gradually you become aware of when a mind state is being controlled by pleasant or unpleasant feelings and if they are causing thoughts, words, and actions that lead to suffering for you or others. At this stage you spontaneously start to realize that you do not have to be controlled by your mind's reaction to pleasant or unpleasant circumstances and react unskillfully. *By coming to know your thoughts and behavior and underlying motivations for them, you develop more skillful behavior.* You move from emotional chaos to clarity, from a reactive mind to a responsive mind.

There are many benefits to becoming more present in the moment. Many people report that they gain the ability to be more spontaneous or to know more fully what action or decision is called for in a situation. Others say that their lives are simply richer. Still others describe feeling truly alive for the first time or more authentic than they have felt since their youth. The feeling of authenticity is a marker of achieving maturity as a human being. Feeling real to yourself and being genuine with others are requirements for sustaining a sense of meaning in life.

Mindfulness can also make you a more effective person in the world. Since you are more present, you notice more about what is going on around you and you see more alternatives for achieving your goals. You also have better access to your intuition and can think more clearly.

A few words of warning: It is easy for your ego to get swept away with its newfound sense of empowerment and lead you to act even more unskillfully, thus defeating the purpose of learning mindfulness. Therefore it is essential that you also develop generosity and ethical standards as you gain personal power. Initially there is also a downside to being more mindful in the moment: It becomes much harder for you to fool yourself. You are stuck with seeing when you are not being who you wish to be. The good news is that by repeatedly observing the suffering you cause by not being your authentic self your behavior starts to change. You reach a point where you cannot stand to see yourself act in such a manner one more time!

At first there may seem to be another downside to mindfulness. As you learn to be more present from moment to moment, you become aware of unpleasant moments that you may have suppressed or ignored in the past. Amazingly, after the initial period of learning to be present, you will discover that mindfulness actually makes unpleasant experiences more bearable because it provides distance from, and understanding of, what's difficult. I often tell students that the clarity of mindfulness is a win-win situation. It gives you a fuller, richer experience of what is pleasant and happy-making in your life while also bringing relief to the difficult and unpleasant. Who can afford to pass up such a gain?

Skillful Living through the Power of Intention

In addition to mindfulness, there is a second life skill that is essential to develop if you are going to move from emotional chaos to clarity: intention. *Intention is the capacity to stay in touch with what is of prime importance to you, from moment to moment, in your daily life.* By "what is of prime importance" I mean those *core values* that you wish to live from as you pursue your life's goals and engage with other people throughout the day. Knowing your intentions allows you to remain authentic and have clarity in meetings at work; interactions with your significant other, family, and friends; and in making decisions about your time, money, and activities.

The fruit of cultivating intention is wisdom. Staying grounded in your intention dramatically shifts how your mind and heart respond to circumstances. It allows your deeper values and your sense of purpose to become the foundation for all your experience. It literally changes *what* you perceive in a situation and how your mind *interprets* what you perceive, and it enhances how you *understand* what you perceive and how you *act* on what you perceive.

For instance, let's say a coworker acts in a manner that is unfair to you. You might perceive this as an act of aggression or a personal attack, which you interpret as a reflection of your unworthiness or your helplessness, and it might even prompt you to become aggressive. You might *react* by either collapsing or lashing out at the other person in an unskillful manner that only makes the situation worse. If you are established in your intentions, however, you may still feel the heat of indignation, but you know you have a choice. You can *respond* in a wise manner—choose to be firm or even aggressive, to ignore it, or to deal with it in some other way. Moreover, because you know your intention and what you are about, you can stay genuine in the situation, despite pressure, uncertainty, and vulnerability. Best of all, the episode does not ruin your day. You are in touch with your intention to not let your mind be tugged back and forth by every single pleasant or unpleasant event; you are clear that your inner experience is what matters to you, not the words of someone reacting like a jerk.

You can begin to see that intention requires mindfulness. It is the ability to be awake in the moment that allows you to stay in touch with your core values and pause before lapsing into a reactive mind state. And when you add intention to mindfulness in your daily activity, the result is a sense of genuineness and authenticity. You know who you are, what you are about, and what matters. During conflicts you act from your inner feelings rather than feelings elicited by the behavior of others. You are comfortable with yourself, and this adds to the feeling of being authentic. Can you see why your wisdom would flourish under such circumstances and why your life would have far greater clarity?

The Art and Science of Skillful Living

Learning to live more skillfully through mindfulness and wise intention is part science and part art, part psychology and part spirituality, part common sense and part envisioning. It is a science in that you objectively identify and develop the skills needed and art because learning how to focus your attention in the various moments of your life involves subjectivity and intuition. It is part psychology because you are developing a much healthier ego and understanding the subtleness of your mind, and it is part spirituality because your core values are based on what you feel gives life meaning. It is common sense because you apply your mindfulness judiciously, not getting lost in overinterpreting what is occurring in the mind, and envisioning because you have to see the possibility that there is genuine opportunity to change your life.

You, just as you are, not some new-and-improved version of yourself, have the opportunity to function at a new level. But it requires your attention, your willingness to reflect and investigate, and, most of all, it requires that you open your heart to its innate yearning to live more skillfully. Skillfulness in living does not come just because you wish you had it or regret that you don't. It is active engagement that brings about change. Skillful living through mindfulness and intention ultimately allows wisdom to blossom. All your mistakes and unskillful moments become fertilizer for your wisdom to grow. You cannot practice wisdom, but you can practice being more skillful!

Everyday Meditation: A Nine-Minute Daily Practice

Joseph Goldstein

The Buddhist path has been illuminated for millennia by monastics, yogis, and others who devote themselves full-time, for a lifetime, to meditation and study. Joseph Goldstein, one of the founders of the Insight Meditation Society, is such a practitioner. Yet he recognizes how difficult it is for the rest of us to find the time for meditation, and he offers us this short but powerful practice we can incorporate into our busy lives.

Recently I was thinking about some close friends who are younger than I am, raising families, with busy lives in the world. I could appreciate that it might be quite some time before they would be able to sit a long retreat. So I started wondering if there was a way for people in those circumstances to integrate some kind of meditation technique into their daily activities that could really touch the transformative power of the practice. On longer retreats it's easier to access meditative depths, but when we're otherwise intensely engaged, it can be quite a challenge.

The foundation of the Buddha's path to liberation is known as right understanding, and it consists of two main strands. One is the understanding and application of the teachings on the law of karma—that is, that our actions have consequences. Seeing this, we undertake the practice of generosity and the practice of the precepts. We take care with what we do so that we're creating conditions for happiness rather than suffering, both for ourselves and others. This strand is frequently talked about, and it covers a lot of what people who are committed to the path usually practice.

But in the context of one's daily life, the second strand is more difficult to work with. This is the basic understanding of *anatta*, or "no-self"—the absence of an inherently existing self. In Pali, the language of the oldest written Buddhist teachings, the belief in some core notion of self is called *sakkaya-ditthi*; this is sometimes translated as "personality belief." It's said to be the most dangerous of all the defilements, more dangerous than greed or even hatred, because these are rooted in this mistaken belief. This wrong view of self is central to how we go about in the world, and all kinds of unskillful actions come out of it.

Of course, the Buddha is talking about the unwholesome effects of acting out of this wrong view—this personality view—not only in terms of one life, but of many lifetimes. It's an extremely powerful conditioning force. And the aim of the practice, central to everything we're doing, is to free the mind from this misconception.

So the question then arose: how can we really address this issue as laypeople caught up in our day-to-day activities? Quite spontaneously a nine-minute-a-day plan came to me, a way to "turbo-charge" our practice by doing three short meditations a day, each three minutes long. Each of these sessions targets a particular area of identification where the mistaken sense of self is created and strengthened.

Session I: Who Is Knowing?

During the first three-minute session we simply sit and listen to sounds, in whatever surroundings we find ourselves. It makes no difference whether we're on a noisy street or in a quiet room. As we open and relax into the awareness of the various sounds, we ask ourselves a question: "Can I find what's knowing these sounds?" Clearly, we're aware of them. But can we find what is knowing? When we investigate, we see there's nothing to find. There's no knower, even though knowing is happening.

This seems a very straightforward way of loosening and hopefully breaking the identification with the knowing as a knower. All that's going on is just hearing. There's no "I" behind it. No knower can be found.

So that's the first three-minute exercise: listen to sounds, see if you can find what's knowing them, and then explore the experience of not being able to find a knower, even though knowing is still there.

Session II: Breaking Identification with the Body

The second three minutes helps break through the very deep identification with the body. For this there are two exercises that could be alternated, or the time could be divided between them.

The friends I had in mind had both lost one parent recently, so the focus of one session is to reflect on anyone we know who has died. If we were with them during that process, what was happening as they were dying, during their last days? Or if we don't have this personal experience, we can reflect on the great sweep of generations over time, that birth inevitably ends in death. Really try to take in the truth of the body dying, take in what our bodies are and what happens to them. This is something that will come to pass for us all.

The idea of this exercise is to reflect on dying in as vivid a way as possible, and to apply it to our partner, to our children, to our friends—seeing that this is what naturally happens to all of us. It isn't morbid, but rather a way of keeping front and center the truth that we all die. This can serve as a powerful reminder that our body is not "self." It is simply going through its own process. One day, it's going to decay and die—that's nature. It's just how it is.

The other exercise for loosening identification with the body is carried out in motion. When I walk somewhere, for example, if I'm mindful and really feeling the body moving, I notice that I'm simply experiencing sensations in space—pressure, motion, lightness. That's all that's happening. There's not the sense of a solid body, and certainly not the sense of an "I" that's doing the walking.

When sensations in space are being known, through the act of walking or any other movement, we begin to get a sense of the body as a fluid energy field. This can be illuminating—it can free the mind from being caught in the notion of the solidity of the body.

These two approaches are a good way of weakening the identification with the body as being self.

Session III: As the Thought Arises . . .

The last area where we get caught a lot in terms of self is the identification with our thoughts. We have thousands of thoughts a day, most of which are casual and low-key. Often we're not even aware of them. And almost all have to do with self—our activities, our future projects, our memories, and the imagined events that involve us.

During an earlier retreat, I noticed that this more subtle stream of thought is like a dream state, and the thought arose, "I'm just dreaming myself into existence." Reflecting on this in the time since then, I see that we're continually dreaming ourselves into existence because we're not aware of thoughts as they're coming through. So the sense of self is continually being reinforced.

For the third three minutes, then, we simply watch for thoughts arising and passing, as we often do in meditation, but with a further turbo-charge: we pay more careful attention so that we're right there, precisely as the thought arises. If the awareness is sharp, we'll observe a thought arise and vanish in the moment. That experience repeatedly weakens the identification with thought. We discover that there's hardly anything there, just a wisp. In our normal lives, with our usual level of attention, we're not conscious of this. But for three minutes we can bring in enough focus so that we actually see it.

This is what I call "the nine-minute-a-day, turbo-charged path to enlightenment." It's important to add, though, that nine minutes a day by itself won't be enough. It needs to be built into the foundation of a daily meditation practice, together with the cultivation of the first strand of right understanding mentioned earlier: the awareness that our actions have consequences. If this nine-minute-a-day program is combined with other aspects of a daily practice, then I believe it can really enliven our understanding of how to apply the teachings in the midst of a very busy life.

Breaking Through

Ezra Bayda

Meditation is easy to learn but hard to do. After all, we are seeking to liber-
ate ourselves from the imprisoning habits of a lifetime, if not much longer.
Fortunately, Buddhist practitioners over the centuries have identified the
obstacles we will encounter on the path of meditation and developed ways
to get past them. Zen teacher Ezra Bayda analyzes three common mistakes
we can make on our meditative journey.

Detours and obstacles are a fact of practice life. Some arise out of
our own psychology and conditioning: patterns of self-judgment
and perfectionism, a tendency to procrastinate or seek diversions,
addiction to control, and the like. Other obstacles seem to be more
universal, and these are the ones that nearly every practitioner faces
at one time or another. These obstacles are at the heart of practice,
yet they are seldom given the emphasis they deserve. But until we
can see them clearly—see how they manifest in our lives—it will be
difficult, if not impossible, for our practice to move forward.

There are three obstacles in particular that we need to address.

Misunderstanding the Depth of Waking Sleep

The first obstacle to practice is not understanding the magnitude
and power of waking sleep. "Waking sleep" refers to the state in

which we live most of the time—identified with, or lost in, our thoughts, our emotions, and our actions. In the first place, we're addicted to our thoughts: believing that our thoughts and opinions are the truth is the veil through which we perceive reality. But we also have difficulty controlling our emotions; in fact, we love to indulge them. Furthermore, we can't seem to stay in the present moment for more than a few seconds at a time; the present is the last place we want to be. Because we are so frequently lost in the obscuring confusion of our thoughts and emotions, we lack the clarity and presence that come when we are more awake.

Buddhism teaches that we are all born with buddhanature and that our spiritual aspiration is to allow our true nature to reveal itself, just as an acorn aspires to become an oak tree. Yet emphasizing our basic goodness, as important as it is, is only part of the picture. No matter how strong our aspiration may be, if we don't develop deep insight into the power and magnitude of waking sleep, we will be blindsided by it again and again. It's imperative for us to understand that spiritual practice is not just something we do when we're sitting in meditation or when we're on retreat. Just as there is no end to the power of waking sleep, there can be no end to practice. Living a practice life means practicing at all times, with everything we encounter, not just when we're on the cushion or when something upsets us. Failing to see everything as an opportunity for practice is a setup for frustration and disappointment, keeping us stuck where we are and limiting our possibilities for inner growth. The more we include in our practice, the more satisfying our life can be.

Underestimating Resistance

The second obstacle we encounter in practice, closely related to the first, is underestimating the degree to which resistance is a predictable and inevitable part of a practice life. Resistance comes in many forms: not wanting to sit in meditation, not wanting to stay with our experience for more than a few seconds, spinning off into thinking about the past or the future, suppressing or avoiding emotional pain, finding fault with ourselves, finding fault with others. We can see resistance in our commitment to believing such thoughts as "This is too hard," "I can't do it," or "I'm unworthy."

Yet another, more subtle form of resistance is thinking and talking about practice rather than actually experiencing our life. Thinking and talking about practice are easy substitutes for the real effort that a practice life requires. We resist facing life as it is because that would mean abandoning our views of how we think it should be. The most basic form of resistance is wanting life to be other than it is.

For the most part, we don't really want to wake up. We have to be honest about this. We want to hold on to our beliefs and even to our suffering. Afraid of the unknown, we cling to the familiar. We don't want to give up our illusions even when they make us miserable. Resistance is the ego's effort to maintain control. Yet no matter what form it takes, it brings us no peace. Pema Chödrön tells a story about a friend who as a child had recurring nightmares in which ferocious monsters were chasing her through a house. Whenever she closed a door behind her, the monsters would burst through the door and frighten her. Pema once asked what the monsters looked like, but her friend couldn't tell her, because in the dream she had never turned around to see.

At some point, however, she decided not to turn away from what she feared. The next time she had the nightmare, just as she was about to open a door to avoid being caught by the monsters, she stopped running, turned around, and looked the monsters in the eye. They were huge, with horrible features, but they didn't attack her; they just jumped up and down. As she looked closer, the three-dimensional multicolored monsters began to shrink into two-dimensional black-and-white shapes. At that moment, the girl awoke, and she never had that nightmare again.

It is in running away from our "monsters" that we make them seem so solid. Whatever we resist exerts a strong hold on us: in solidifying it, we empower it to stay in our mind and our life. But when we cultivate the willingness to be with life just as it is, our relationship to what we've avoided starts to change. Once we see through the solidity of our resistance, our lives become more fluid and work-able. We're able to move beyond where we were once stuck. Even if we don't like our life as it is, we don't need to wage war against it. We can start meeting our resistance squarely by noticing all of the ways in which we avoid the present moment, the ways in which we avoid practice, the ways in which we resist what is. Understanding the depth of our resistance is of major importance in furthering our practice.

Another form of resistance arises when we hit the "dry spot." The dry spot is the moment when we lose our connection with the aspiration that originally brought us to practice. Often we hit the dry spot when our expectations of practice are unfulfilled—when it isn't bringing us the immediate peace, calm, or freedom from fear that we had hoped for. Disappointment leads to anger, and anger to resistance.

It's important to understand, however, that vacillating between aspiration and resistance is the natural rhythm of practice and that the dry spot is a natural manifestation of this cycle. But the first few times we hit the dry spot, it doesn't seem natural at all. We may even feel as if we're failing at practice, since the thoughts that arise in these moments seem like fixed truths. It's hard to see them for what they are—simply automatic reactions to the inevitable ups and downs of practice life.

Hitting the dry spot is the point at which students often leave practice. But if we can wait it out, we begin to understand the natu-ral cycle of resistance. We even come to expect the doubting mind to arise. Doubt in itself is not the problem. The problem comes from identifying with the doubting "me" and believing that this is who we really are. But if seen for what it is, doubt can even be a positive force in practice. Provided we don't get lost in the negative beliefs that arise with it, it can lead to a deepening of our quest. As practice takes hold, we can learn to use doubt as an opportunity to experience the grief of our unfulfilled expectations about practice. We can learn to surrender to, and reside in, the physical experience of what doubt feels like in the body, instead of following the story line of negative thoughts. Not following the story line can be difficult, because the thoughts seem so true, so solid, so compelling. But if we can stay with the visceral experience of doubt, even as the anguish of not knowing remains, the dryness is transfused with a deeper sense of aspiration.

Thomas Merton expressed this clearly: "True love and prayer are learned in the moment when prayer has become impossible and the heart has turned to stone." When we understand the cycles of resistance and can wait out a dry period by resting in the direct physical experience of doubt, we will gradually come to feel a renewed sense of direction and hope.

WANTING TO FEEL A PARTICULAR WAY

The third major obstacle we encounter in practice is a deep-seated desire to feel a particular way, whether calm or clear or spacious or simply free of anxiety. Probably all of us share the illusion that if we practice long enough and hard enough, we'll get what we want: enlightenment, good health, a satisfying relationship, or whatever else we're seeking. We can tell that we're still harboring this illusion if we believe that experiencing difficulties or distress means that something is wrong—specifically, that something is wrong with us. This persistent belief drives us to do whatever we can to alleviate our discomfort. We believe deeply that if we just practice harder, we're sure to feel better.

We should never underestimate the extent to which we equate feeling better with being awake. But a key point about spiritual practice is that we don't have to feel any particular way. Nor do we have to be any particular way. All we can do is experience, and work with, whatever is arising in our life right now. No matter what is going on or how we feel about it, the essence of practice is to honestly acknowledge whatever is happening in the moment and stay present with our experience of it. In this way we can come to feel a true appreciation for life just as it is.

There's a famous Buddhist story about a man who was shot in

the chest with an arrow. The pain was great, but the Buddha pointed out to the man how much greater the pain would be if he had been shot with a second arrow in the exact same spot. What this teaching suggests is that however painful or disappointing our experience may be, adding the second arrow of our judgmental thoughts about it will only deepen the pain and lead to greater suffering.

If, for example, I wake up not feeling well, adding the judgment "This shouldn't be happening to me" will only make me feel much worse. The countermeasure to judging is to move out of the mental world and our thoughts about what's happening, and into the physical realm and what we're actually feeling in the moment. Judgments are based on ideals or expectations, and these thought-based pictures are at least one step removed from what is real. Coming back to what is, minus our thought-based pictures, is a step toward freedom.

When we can see through our deep-seated desire to feel a particular way and realize that we don't have to feel different in order to be free, we can experience the equanimity that comes with staying truly present with what is.

Fully grasping the three obstacles that we're sure to encounter on the spiritual path—misunderstanding the depth of waking sleep, underestimating resistance, and wanting to feel a particular way—is the essential foundation for learning how to work with them effectively. And working with them, in turn, will take us to the heart of what it means to be free.

Not Quite Nirvana

Rachel Neumann

Sometimes the most helpful things we learn don't come from teachers but from people like us, just struggling to do the best they can with this life. Rachel Neumann is a student of Thich Nhat Hanh's who has edited many of his books. Working to apply his teachings in her own life, she has learned some lessons about listening we can all benefit from.

Often when I ask my daughter Plum to take a deep breath, she responds, "I can breathe while I talk!" Until recently, I had that same attitude about listening. I can listen while I talk! I can listen while I think about my grocery list or the bump on my forehead! In my work as a book editor, I was learning to really listen to what I was reading, reading it a few times, saying it to myself and, as I usually had questions and there was no one to ask them to, going back and reading again. This was hard enough with text that just sat there, without interrupting or judging me, but listening that way to other live human beings, whose words are always mixed with their own questions, emotions, and judgments, was proving to be a lot harder.

One of the reasons we spend so little time being available to ourselves or others is that listening, really listening, can be inconvenient and time-consuming. We all think that we listen better than other people. It's true, other people aren't very good listeners. It's true, we're not. I'm not. I tend to talk and think really fast; when other people talk, I tend to jump ahead to the end of their sentences in my mind. I sometimes am so busy trying not to interrupt them with the answer to what they're clearly working their way to asking that I forget that they're talking and start doing something else, like cutting my nails or checking my e-mail. It's not pretty.

Thich Nhat Hanh and I recently spent a year working on a book about fidelity and the success of long-term relationships. It's a 150-page book, but I'll give you the secret here in just a couple of lines. If you want to make your relationship work, be honest about your own suffering and prejudices. Take the time for yourself to pay attention to the itch or bump or the grocery list, so it's not popping up when your partner is talking. In other words, only listen when you're available.

For my partner Jason and I, this has meant less time pretending to listen and a little more time actually listening. It turned out that although I've always thought I was pretty good at pretend listening, he could tell. He knew I was just impatiently waiting for him to finish so I could get my advice in. It turns out that listening is like meditating; it's painful, especially in the beginning, and shouldn't be done for long periods of time.

One time, when Jason was talking about a client of his, and I was giving him good advice, he stopped me. "I don't want your advice," he said. "I just want you to listen." I glared at him. "Then you should have told me at the beginning," I said. "I would have listened differently!" He glared back at me, but after that we have each learned to say, before talking about something hard, "Are you available to listen?" It's amazing how, if I'm asked outright, I'm able to just listen in a way that I didn't know was even a possibility before.

Sometimes, I can't listen. I'm tired or distracted or the day has just been too much. Then I am learning to say "No." It's disappointing and irritating, but it's better, I've found, than pretending. One of the difficulties for me in deep listening is I am impatient to find answers and make things better. If I just listen, I worry that listening will be considered "enough" and that things will never change. It's trust that I'm slowly building, in Jason and in myself, that deep listening may or may not be enough, but that it is almost always the first step.

I believe strongly in snap judgments, critical thinking, and sweeping generalities, and I've struggled to accept that listening deeply doesn't mean giving up these things. Given the way human brains have been set up to discern and edit, listening without judgment is impossible. Sitting and breathing with awareness helps, in that I'm taking time for myself; at least I'm meditating. Sitting still, it's easier to see the thoughts come and go without getting too swept up in them. But as soon as I'm done, it's back to functioning, also known as judgment.

I'm still figuring out how to listen deeply and still function with the level of quick reflexes and intensity my life requires. I think Thich Nhat Hanh would say I should slow down. But I don't have any desire for more slowness. Instead, I am working on listening without immediately acting on or giving much weight to the judgment that occurs. It's useful to acknowledge the judgments I'm making all the time. Then I can see where they come from. Sometimes, I look and decide I'm right on: this or that person or idea is a wanker. Other times, usually two minutes too late, I realize all my righteousness is coming from my own fear or anger or craving and I'm deeply embarrassed.

With friends, I find it easy to step back. With Jason, it's getting easier. But when it comes to my children, as they've gotten older, I find deep listening to be really difficult. Perhaps this is because I've known them since I could listen to them without words, and now they're full of words that often distract me from what they're feeling. Partly this is because I also have my own childhood experiences that color how I see theirs. Listening to them is a lot harder than taking care of them, coordinating for them, and showering them with affection. It's because when I listen, I feel like I have to *do* something about it.

This morning, Luna, my oldest daughter, wanted to throw a slug she found on the front steps into the city compost bucket. Usually, she gets ten cents for every slug she throws in, and five for every snail. But this morning, we were late for school, and we didn't have time for the slug ritual. I told her we had to leave the slug for now, and it would either be there when she got back from school or (hopefully) eaten by a blackbird.

This was not okay. Luna began with what I guess is the most common refrain of all school-age children. "It's not fair," she said. She loved that slug, and it might get smooshed if we just left it there on the sidewalk. She needed that ten cents and was going to buy something with it. She continued to chant "It's not fair" over and over again, for the first ten minutes of the car ride. For two minutes, I was irritated. She was being unreasonable. But then I got into her chant, took each sentence as an opportunity to listen and to breathe, and started enjoying it. After a few minutes, I was done. I informed her that she could keep going, but I'd heard she didn't think it was fair and now I was going to listen to the radio. She continued for another five minutes, though in a softer tone, enjoying the sound of her own complaint.

Recently, all the parents of second graders at Luna's school were called in for a meeting about our children. We sat there listening as the psychologists introduced themselves and talked about the social and emotional development of eight-year-olds and their growing development of hierarchies. Finally, a parent anxiously burst out with what many of us were thinking, "But why are we here?" What did we do? Before we could listen to anything, we needed to know: Are we in trouble? Did we do something wrong?

We get irritated when our children are upset, not just because we love them and want them to be happy. If that was all, we'd be sad when they're sad, but we wouldn't get so angry or frustrated. We get upset because we often feel we have to fix it and we can't. We can't make the other kid at the park share his toys, and we can't make a snack out of thin air when they are hungry in the car. Or we get upset because something similar happened to us and we had the same feeling, but we weren't able to take care of it. Now here it is again in front of us.

There is so little we can actually fix. I know this with little things.

Once we were driving, there was no way we were going to go back and deposit the slug, so I could relax about it. There was nothing to do. It's harder when Plum tells me she is terrified of dying or when Luna says she is lonely on the schoolyard. These are things that trigger my own memories and anxieties. It's hard to want to hear it unless I can fix it.

Big or small, listening is still the biggest percentage of what I can actually do. The smaller, but still important part, is the judgment and figuring out what action needs to happen. Once I started listening to what Thich Nhat Hanh was actually trying to say, there was a lot of structural editing that I needed to do. As an editor I went from being the housecleaner to the demolition and construction crew. The more space I gave to listening, the clearer my understanding of what I needed to do next.

The Buddha encouraged all of his listeners to cultivate the three energies of mindfulness (*smrti* in Sanskrit), concentration (*samadhi*) and insight (*prajna*). I'd always thought the words looked beautiful together, and sounded good, but their connection was beginning to make sense when I tried it. Mindfulness (open awareness, availability) leads to concentration (deep listening, focus) leads to insight (clarity and understanding of what to do next).

Although there were many advantages of having hippie parents (Play in the dirt! Eat the dirt! Make your own yogurt! Fall asleep while the grownups dance to Bob Marley!), one disadvantage is they were bigger on light listening than on action. As a child, all I wanted was for my parents to punch the gut of the kid who was bullying me, or at least teach me how to make a tight fist. When my parents seemed to listen only to tell me how sorry they were, instead of feeling listened to I just felt stuck and helpless. I didn't just want empathy; I wanted to be safe at school and in my own home.

So I can overreact and err on the other side, skipping the listening and jumping on my horse and grabbing my sword to slay the bully before my children are finished telling their story. I'm working on the balance.

Here's my goal: Listen deeply. Ask questions. Then stop for a moment. Check again on my availability. Then if necessary, let judgment lead to action. Let my kids come up with their own insights. If necessary, give them a leg up on the horse, lend them my sword, and push them in the right direction. I'll ride backup, just in case they need someone to listen to them as they go.

The Power of Gone

Shinzen Young

The basis of Buddhist meditation is precise, moment-by-moment observation of whatever arises in our experience. By watching carefully, with a stable mind, we gain insight into the nature of reality as it unfolds before us. Buddhist teacher Shinzen Young suggests this variation on vipassana, *or insight meditation, in which we focus on the inevitable dissolving of thoughts, perceptions, and emotions.*

And until you know of this:
How to grow through death
You're just another troubled guest,
On the gloomy earth.
　　—JOHANN WOLFGANG VON GOETHE, "Holy Longing"

My students sometimes ask me, "Is there a quickest path to enlightenment?" My standard answer is, "Perhaps, but I don't think it's currently known by humanity. In our current stage of spiritual science, different approaches seem to work for different people. That's why I like to give you folks a wide range of contrasting techniques to choose from."

Then, recently, I decided to do a thought experiment. What if I were only allowed to teach one focus technique and no other?

Which technique would I pick? It was a difficult choice, but I finally concluded that it would be a technique I call "Just Note Gone."

Most people are aware of the moment when a sensory event starts but seldom aware of the moment when it vanishes. We are instantly drawn to a new sound or new sight or new body sensation, but seldom notice when the previous sound, sight, or body sensation disappears. This is natural, because each new arising represents what we need to deal with in the next moment. But to always be aware of sensory arisings and hardly ever be aware of sensory passings creates an unbalanced view of the nature of sensory experience.

To practice the "Just Note Gone" technique, follow these basic instructions: Whenever a sensory experience—a sound, a sight, a body sensation—suddenly disappears, make a note of it. Clearly acknowledge when you detect the transition point between all of it being present and at least some of it no longer being present. You can use the mental label "gone" to help you note the end of the experience. If nothing vanishes for a while, that's fine. Just hang out until something does. If you start worrying about the fact that nothing is ending, note each time that thought ends. There is only a finite amount of real estate available in consciousness at any given instant. Each arising somewhere causes a passing somewhere else.

So what? Why should we care about whether we can detect the moment when a particular burst of mental talk or a particular external sound or a particular body sensation suddenly subsides? Suppose you had to go through some horrible experience that involved physical pain, emotional distress, mental confusion, and perceptual disorientation all at once. Where could you turn for safety? Where could you turn for comfort? Where could you turn for meaning? Turning toward your body won't help. There's nothing but pain and fear there. Turning toward your mind won't help. There's nothing but confusion and uncertainty there. Turning toward sight and sound won't help. There's nothing but turmoil and chaos there.

Under such extreme duress, is there anywhere you can turn to find relief? Yes. You can concentrate intently on the fact that each sensory insult passes. In other words, you can reverse the normal habit of turning to each new arising and instead turn to each new passing. Micro-relief is constantly available.

There are some reasonable objections to this way of looking at things. For one thing, it might seem too extreme to be relevant. After all, most people on most days don't have to face all-encompassing horror. That's true. However, most people will probably experience a deeply painful experience at some point in their lives. It would be a source of great comfort to know, based on one's own direct experience, that there is a place of safety so deep that nothing can touch it.

How much can micro-endings help? It depends. Depends on what? It depends on three things: sensory clarity (the ability to detect moments of vanishing), concentration power (the ability to stay focused on moments of vanishing), and inner equanimity (the ability to allow sensory experiences to come and go without push and pull).

You can think of equanimity as the ability to quickly and deeply say "Yes!" to each new sensory arising. Quick and deep openness to an experience facilitates quick and deep goneness of that experience. This creates a positive feedback mechanism. The more equanimity you have at arisings, the easier it is to detect passings. The more you detect passings, the easier it is to have equanimity at arisings. This loop exponentially accelerates your learning.

With time, the "Just Note Gone" technique will sensitize you to detect vanishings more clearly. This, combined with the equanimity loop, makes it possible to concentrate continuously on vanishings. This in turn transforms micro-ending into mega-relief.

Noting "gone" produces other positive effects in addition to a sense of relief. Some people find that noticing moments of vanishing creates a deep sense of restfulness. Visual, auditory, or somatic tranquility may seem to propagate through consciousness whenever you notice a "gone." Each moment of cessation points to absolute rest—the still point of the turning world.

Noting "gone" allows you to experience "This too is passing," which will provide more comfort than if you just try to remind yourself "This too shall pass." Noting "gone" creates a stillness and tranquility within you; this is a natural consequence of the nature of vanishing.

But there is another effect that people often report and that seems to go against the nature of vanishing. Some people find noting "gone" to be rich and sensory-fulfilling. Where things go to is where things come from. Each time you note "gone," for a brief instant your attention is pointed directly toward the richness of the Source. That is what's behind the seeming paradox of satisfying nothingness. There is a word that means both "cessation" and "satisfaction" as a single linked concept. The word is "nirvana."

Noting "gone" may also lead to a spontaneous spirit of love and service (*bodhichitta*). As you come to know the source of your own consciousness, you also come to know the source of everyone's consciousness—the shared formless womb of all beings. Noting "gone" can lead to a spontaneous sense of oneness with (and commitment to) all beings. So goneness, although it may seem cold and impersonal, is actually deeply connected to the issue of human fulfillment and human goodness.

As you become more sensitive to detecting "gone," you may come to a place where you note it so frequently that goneness itself becomes an object of high concentration. The gaps between the vanishings get shorter and shorter until goneness becomes the stable ground. Self and world become fleeting figures. People sometimes ask me why I don't make breath the centerpiece of meditation, as many teachers do. There seems to be a general impression that the ultimate goal of mindfulness practice is to be able to stay focused on the breath. I sometimes parody that notion with the slogan "Real meditators are able to come back to the breath." Actually, if you insist that I give you something to always come back to, I would say, "Real meditators are able to come back to 'gone.'"

Are there any possible negative effects from working with vanishing and the related themes of emptiness and no-self? Occasionally there can be. In some cases, the sense of goneness, emptiness, and no-self may be so intense that it creates disorientation, aversion, or hopelessness. Unpleasant reactions such as these are well documented in the classical literature of contemplation from Eastern and Western traditions alike. In the West, it is sometimes referred to as the Dark Night of the Soul. In the East, it is sometimes referred to as the Pit of the Void, or as the unpleasant side of *bhanga* (dissolution). This doesn't happen very often, but if it does, there are three interventions that you can use to transform the situation from being problematic to being blissful.

Accentuate the good parts of the Dark Night, even though they may seem very subtle relative to the bad parts. You may be able to glean some sense of tranquility within the nothingness. There may be some sense of inside and outside becoming one (leading to expanded identity). There may be some soothing, vibratory energy massaging you. There may be a springy, expanding-contracting energy animating you.

Negate the negative parts of the Dark Night by deconstructing them through mindful awareness. Remember "divide and conquer"—if you can divide a negative reaction into its parts (mental image, mental talk, and emotional body sensation), you can conquer the sense of being overwhelmed. In other words, eliminate the negative parts by loving them to death.

Affirm positive emotions, behaviors, and cognitions in a sustained, systematic way. Gradually, patiently, reconstruct a new habitual self through practices such as loving-kindness.

In most cases, all three interventions must be practiced and maintained for however long it takes to get through the Dark Night. It may also require ongoing and intensive support from teachers and other practitioners to remind you to keep applying these interventions. The end result, though, will be a depth of joy and freedom beyond one's wildest imagining. Where things go to is where they come from.

The Third Turning of the Wheel

Reb Anderson

There is an old Chinese saying that describes the Buddhist path. Perhaps you know it: First there is a mountain; then there is no mountain; then there is a mountain again. What has happened over that journey? How does the reality we return to differ from the reality where we started? These three steps are also called the Buddha's three turnings of the wheel of dharma. Reb Anderson, an important American Zen teacher, explains how they unfold.

A buddha is someone who sees the way things really are. When we see the way things really are, we see that we're all in this together, that we are all interdependent. A great surpassing love arises from that wisdom, and that love leads a buddha to wish that all beings would open to this wisdom and be free of the misery that arises from ignoring the way things are. Buddhas appear in the world because they want us to have a buddha's wisdom, so that we will love every single being completely and protect every single being without exception and without limit—just as all the buddhas do.

The *Samdhinirmocana Sutra* shows us how Shakyamuni Buddha sought to fulfill this wonderful desire, how he tries to bring us all to enlightenment. The scripture tells us that the Buddhist tradition has three phases, or as it is usually put, that there are three turnings of the wheel of dharma. What many believe to be the first scripture recording Shakyamuni Buddha's actual words is called the *Dharmachakra Parvartana,* or "Setting the Wheel of the Dharma in Motion." There were two more turnings of the wheel, and the *Samdhinirmocana Sutra* speaks of both of them.

Buddha taught in different ways for different audiences, and the threads of the teachings sometimes got entangled with each other because they weren't laid out systematically. People sometimes got confused about what the teaching was. So this sutra attempts to straighten the threads out.

THE FIRST TURNING

When the historical Buddha appeared in the world, there was something about him in his enlightened condition that made people ask him to teach them. People would ask him, "What's going on with you? Why do you look so serene and joyful?" So the Buddha, with his intention to liberate all beings, interacted with people who had their own intentions and perspectives, and when they interacted, various things came up. He had to speak in a language that the people listening to him could understand, so in this first turning of the dharma wheel he offered a conceptual, logical teaching. He showed us how to analyze our experience, and he set out a path for people to find freedom and liberate themselves from suffering.

The goal of this analysis was to show us that our life experience is fleeting, impermanent, and unstable. But the Buddha didn't usually just tell people that their lives were fleeting, unstable, and impermanent. He usually emphasized a way of looking at experience so that the fleeting, unstable quality of life would be discovered. And he taught this analysis so that we would see not only that our experience is fleeting, but also that there is no receptacle, or container, or supervisor, or controller, or possessor, or pilot in addition to the fleeting elements shown by the analysis.

This process of analysis also looks at the different moral qualities of our experience to see whether our behavior is tainted or pure. Tainted means different things to different people, but the question is simply: is our activity, our living right now, oriented toward gain and loss? We look to see whether our activity is oriented toward gain and loss or is free of concern for gain and loss. This analysis of the moral dimension also reveals that the concern for gain and loss is based on the idea of self, but there is actually no independent self in this field of experience. If I see that what I'm doing is concerned with gain, I will discover that I think there is a controller, a supervisor, a possessor, a container of the multiplicity of elements of my experience. And because I think that, I'm concerned with gain and loss for that controller, for that owner, for that independent self, and that makes me suffer.

The more we analyze our experience, the more we see this idea of an independent self that arises with concern for gain and loss, and the more we come to see that such a self cannot be detected in actual experience. There is the idea of a controller, but the controller cannot be found. There is the idea of a container of our experience, but the container cannot be found. There is an idea of an owner of our experience, but no owner can be found. "Owner" goes with concern for gain and loss and turmoil and suffering. "No owner" goes with no concern for gain and loss and with true freedom. This is what the early teachings of the Buddha were about.

We can also look at what helps us pay attention to what's going on, and this too helps disabuse us of the idea of independent existence. This analysis purifies the mindstream. It helps us see more and more clearly the absence of anything permanent or independent. This first turning of the wheel was addressed to the person looking at self; someone looking at her own experience, purifying herself through moral analysis and through the analysis of empirical experience, and becoming personally liberated in that process. The first turning was personal and conceptual, and it produced individual liberation. As things came up in his interaction with people, the

Buddha was happy to teach individual people this logical conceptual path to personal liberation. It was a path that helped people become free of suffering and live in the world as a pure experiential event. It helped them drop the belief that they were separate from other beings or, for that matter, that they had any independent existence at all. The first turning of the wheel was for the purpose of individual liberation, and the Buddha was quite successful. Many people who listened to this teaching, understood this teaching, practiced this teaching, became purified of their false beliefs, and won personal liberation.

You could say the Buddha was a revolutionary, but you could also say he was a great flowering of the Indian religious tradition. One Sanskrit scholar told me that if you look at all the words the Buddha used in his teachings, you find that almost none of them were new. Wherever he was, he used the language of the culture. The only new word the Buddha used that wasn't just common Indian religious language was "bodhisattva"—that one word. Otherwise he was using the words of the culture. He shared a lot with other yogis. You can see he had great yogic powers, but others had yogic powers, too. He could see where people were coming from and where they were going, but other yogis could, too. But his interpretation of this process of change—particularly in terms of his understanding of the self—was a little bit different from everyone else's. As far as we know, nothing like it had been seen before. And the way it was taught after his death became even more subtle still. People in India during Buddha's time weren't ready to hear all the implications of his doctrine of no-self. Later, after the Buddhist community had taken deep root, we have the second turning of the wheel, which presents even more profound and more subtle teachings on selflessness.

Avalokiteshvara, speaking on behalf of the Buddha in the *Heart of Perfect Wisdom Sutra*, said that "all dharmas are marked by emptiness" (*sarva-dharmah sunyata-lakasana*). All dharmas, all phenomena, are empty. But in the second turning of the wheel, this teaching on emptiness is vastly expanded. A hidden implication of this and all the Buddha's other teachings is that, like all things, the teaching itself is an interdependent phenomenon. He's giving it to you because you're the one he's talking to, but ultimately there's no reality in what he's saying. It is just something that comes up between you like a dance. And because it's interdependently arising, it has no ultimate existential status. But he didn't explicitly say that at first. People might have said, "Well then, why should we listen to you?" Or they might have said, "Why should we practice the moral precepts, if they have no ultimate, existential status?"

The Buddha had to establish a strong ethical foundation for his students before he could encourage them to meditate on the selflessness of all phenomena, and many people did attain personal liberation with such ethically grounded meditation. But until practitioners are deeply grounded ethically, buddhas do not bring up the more subtle wisdom teachings that might undermine the ethical foundation of the community of practitioners.

In the Buddha's first scripture he begins with the wisdom teachings of the Middle Way and the four noble truths and not with teachings on ethical commitment and discipline. I believe the reason he could do this for his first students was that they were already very well grounded in ethical discipline, and they had realized deep concentration practices based on that ethical ground. Upon this foundation, it was appropriate for the Buddha to offer them wisdom teachings.

Over the millennia, Buddhism has become very strong in terms of ethical discipline and the monastic systems to uphold it, but the danger of losing sight of our ethical foundations remains. As we get into more and more subtle realms of truth, and realize that morality is empty of inherent existence, we might not be able to uphold the commitment and rigors of moral discipline unless that realization is mature. And if we can't continue to be wholeheartedly devoted to ethical discipline while we go into the study of the profound emptiness of things, then we should stop opening to the ultimate truth of emptiness.

THE SECOND TURNING

When the Buddha passed into complete nirvana, the community was strong, and there were many enlightened disciples. But the Buddhist community had to become still more mature before it could withstand the impact of the second turning. It took about five hundred years before that next turning occurred. The historical Buddha was no longer alive, and so the next turning of the wheel had to use a different buddha. A cosmic buddha was going to have to turn the wheel. And the cosmic buddha did not emphasize that what is happening is impermanent, fleeting, bouncing, dancing elements, as in the first turning, but taught that these elements have no independent existence. The second turning offers no conceptual approach to reality. It refutes the previous method and the previous path based on a conceptual approach to liberation. In the *Heart Sutra*, the great cosmic bodhisattva Avalokiteshvara tells us that form, feelings, perceptions, mental formations, and consciousness are all empty, and in emptiness there is no suffering, no cause of suffering, no end of suffering, and no path to freedom from suffering. In other words, none of the Buddha's conceptual teachings, such as the four noble truths and the eightfold path, really apply.

In the first turning of the wheel, things were interdependent and real. In the second turning, they're ultimately empty and unreal because they're interdependent. So there is no logical approach to practice, no approach to liberation, no path to freedom. Because all things are interdependent, including freedom, freedom itself is not real. Suffering is interdependent, and therefore suffering is not ultimately real. In this second turning of the wheel, bondage, turmoil, and misery are interdependent phenomena and therefore not real. Liberation and peace and joy are interdependent and therefore not real. Thus liberation and bondage have the same nature.

This kind of teaching creates problems for some people. But any problems that come up have the nature of being completely free of any problems. The way that things are is right before us, right now, and using any approach to them is a distraction.

Another big difference from the first turning of the wheel is that this pathless path is not about personal liberation. The path where we see that complete freedom and complete bondage have the same nature is not the path of individual liberation; it's the path of liberating all beings. It's not the path of an individual buddha or the historical Buddha; it's the path of a buddha that is the same as the entire universe. The entire universe, in the second turning of the wheel, is always showing us the truth, no matter what's happening. There is no conceptual approach to the entire universe. It just immediately presents itself all the time. And because there's no conceptual approach, there's no difference in access for those who have received instructions about the path and those who haven't. Those who haven't had instructions have no path to drop. Those who have had instructions have a path to drop. The Buddhists and the non-Buddhists are on the same level with this truth. The non-Buddhists don't have to give up Buddhism; the Buddhists do. The non-Buddhists, however, have to give up whatever they've got, because we have to meet what's happening directly with no words, with no concepts. This is the path of universal liberation. This is the second turning.

THE THIRD TURNING

The next path, the third turning of the wheel, which is talked about in this scripture, resurrects the conceptual approach. It offers us a logical path, just like the first one. But this logical path is based on the refutation of the logical path. It's based on the second path, which says, if you take the slightest step toward the truth, you move away from it; if you use any means to realize what you are, you alienate yourself. That's the second path. The second path is actually the truest in a way. But unfortunately it seems to refute all the teachings of Buddha prior to that, and many people found those teachings very, very useful. So the third path redeems the logical approach to practice, but it is a logical approach that is based on the refutation of logic.

The first turning of the wheel constructed a path of liberation, the second turning refutes the path, and the third turning accepts the refutation of the path and redeems the path. This scripture offers a path based on the refutation of the earlier path but redeems the earlier path. Another way to say it is that the first turning gives the logic of liberation, the second condemns all logic, and the third reconstructs logic but based on the understanding that logic is ultimately completely useless. In fact, the third phase used logic more than ever before, and it could use logic more energetically because it was based on the emptiness of logic.

In this sutra, the bodhisattvas ask the Buddha: "You taught this way, the first turning way, and then you taught the second turning way. When you were teaching the second turning, what was your intention?" Then the Buddha explains his intention and that there are these three turnings. The first turning is an analytical, conceptual approach, teaching the five aggregates, the eighteen *dhatus*, the four noble truths, the twelve links of dependent origination, and so on. All these different kinds of teachings aimed to help people see phenomena in such a way that they would be relieved of the belief in the independent existence of the self. Then in the second turning, the Buddha taught that everything, including the teachings, lacks inherent existence, is unproduced, unceasing, and naturally in a state of nirvana. After he gave those teachings, the bodhisattvas said: "That sounds very different from the early teaching. What did you have in mind?" So he tells us what he really had in mind in both cases, which then becomes part of the third turning teaching, which is a deeper revelation of the nature of ultimate truth.

The third turning protects us from a dangerously narrow understanding of the second turning. It's possible that some understandings of the second turning would deprecate the first turning. But a subtle understanding of the second turning enhances the first turning, so that the first turning then can be taught in a more subtle and a more selfless way than it could be taught the first time. When the Buddha Shakyamuni first taught, he allowed the illusion that there was something to get from his dharma. In order to reach some people, he needed to make the teachings look like they really existed. In the second turning, he shows that all the teachings and all the methods only have apparent existence. In the third turning, we find a presentation of the first turning that is in accord with the second turning. So in this scripture, we are offered a systematic path and a conceptual approach that are free of self.

After we realize the ultimate, we see whether we can come back into the conventional, conceptual presentation of the teaching in such a way that we don't violate the understanding of the ultimate truth. We spiral round and round and round until all beings have a correct understanding of the teachings. The wish to do this is called *bodhichitta*—the Way-seeking mind—and the realization of the ability to do that is the fruition of bodhichitta.

There is a Zen saying that goes: "When I first was practicing the Way, there were mountains and rivers. After I practiced for thirty years, I understood there are no mountains and no rivers. Now, finally, there are mountains and rivers again." But these mountains and rivers walk and talk. These mountains and rivers leap through the sky and boogie in the basement. These mountains and rivers are the fully realized mountains and rivers, because these mountains and rivers are based on the understanding that finally there aren't any mountains and rivers. We can't really understand that there are no mountains and rivers until we understand mountains and rivers. We can't really understand mountains and rivers until we understand that there are no mountains and rivers.

So we need these three turnings of the wheel. We need the conceptual approach. We need to enter into an immediacy of our life that gives up the conceptual approach. And then we need a conceptual approach to test that we really have given up the conceptual approach. We need a Zen center with an address, a door, a telephone number, an e-mail address, and a website, with buildings and gardens and robes and hats and people, and especially vegetarian feasts. We need all that, and we need the teachings of the tradition, but then we need to refute the whole thing and have people at the door saying: "This is not a Zen center. There's no Zen center here."

Otherwise, it's not really a Zen center. And then, just to test to see if we really understand that there isn't any Zen center, we take care of the Zen center. But as we take care of it, we ask ourselves: "Are we taking care of it with the understanding that in ultimate truth there is no Zen?"

Of course, sometimes we notice that the way we're taking care of the Zen center looks like we think there really is a Zen center, and there's not much sign that we realize that there's no Zen center. There doesn't seem to be an understanding that this interdependent thing called a Zen center can never be found precisely because it's interdependent. So then we confess, "We don't understand Zen here at Zen center," and that sounds pretty good. But then we also think: "We do understand Zen at Zen center, and we're confident about that because our understanding is based on 'we do not understand Zen at Zen center.'" And we're kind of happy about that because we understand that it's not just us—nobody understands what Zen is. But we may be the ones who are happy about not understanding.

The teaching of the three turnings of the wheel is a conceptual offering to help us understand a nonconceptual approach to liberation or, I should say, to understand no approach to buddhahood, no approach to freedom. It is a conceptual approach to understand no conceptual approach—a conceptual approach to immediacy. And the immediacy is not at all disturbed by being involved in a conceptual approach, because in every moment of being involved in a conceptual approach we are immediately intimate with the ultimate truth of the conceptual approach: namely, that it's not real.

If we don't have a conceptual approach, that's fine, although it's very rare. The main thing is that, as we're involved in our conceptual approach to whatever we're doing, we don't miss the immediate, nonconceptual reality that we can never be separated from. Then we can enjoy ultimate truth no matter what's happening. But this enjoyment is not for yourself. The nonconceptual approach is for the liberation of all beings. The conceptual approach, although it can be quite good, is for the conceiver, and the conceiver doesn't exist.

We aspire to be the Buddha's offspring, and so we are like larva bodhisattvas, but the larvae need a skin. And what's the skin? The skin is the Buddha's conceptual approach. We wrap that little larva in a nice silken conceptual package with neat little analytic, conceptual techniques, and we cook in this cocoon until we shed the conceptual techniques and just be butterflies. And now that we're butterflies, we can teach other larvae about how to put a skin around themselves in a more selfless way, because we're liberated from our conceptual approaches.

When we first come to the practice, in some sense we're like little larvae, since we haven't found our own inner truth yet. So we wrap ourselves in the Buddha's teaching of the first turning. And we grow in that, and then we drop that, and then we just directly be ourselves, our butterfly selves. Then we lay the eggs of the teaching so there can be another generation.

This is the cycle of the wheel. It's the first turning, the second turning, the third turning, the first turning, the second turning, the third turning, and so on. We need to keep cycling our conceptual activity with the immediacy of reality and then test the immediacy of reality by reentering the world of conception, the world of words. Then we drop the words, drop the signs, drop the characteristics, drop the conceptions, and enter into the world of immediate freedom. Then we test it by reentering the world of the manipulation of concepts, and round and round we go.

The Heart Attack Sutra

Karl Brunnhölzl

Legend has it that when the Buddha first taught the great doctrine of emptiness, many of the arhats present had heart attacks on the spot. For what could be more shocking than the discovery that everything we have considered true is actually without substance or ultimate reality? Yet the Buddha then taught another surprising truth: when we realize emptiness, there is bliss. When mind is not obscured by ignorance, there is nothing to fear, no suffering, and nothing to cause suffering. Buddhist scholar Karl Brunnhölzl looks at the famed Heart Sutra *not as abstract philosophy but as the truth of our lives right now.*

There is no doubt that the *Heart Sutra* is the most frequently used and recited text in the entire Mahayana Buddhist tradition, which still flourishes in Japan, Korea, Vietnam, Tibet, Mongolia, Bhutan, China, parts of India and Nepal, and, more recently, also in the Americas and Europe. Many people have said many different things about what the *Heart Sutra* is and what it is not, such as being the heart of wisdom, a statement of how things truly are, the key teaching of the Mahayana, a condensation of all the *Prajnaparamita Sutras* (the Buddha's second turning of the wheel of dharma), or an explanation of emptiness in a nutshell. In order to understand the actual words of the *Heart Sutra*, it's helpful to first explore its background within the Buddhist tradition as well as the meanings of "prajnaparamita" and "emptiness."

One thing we can safely say about the *Heart Sutra* is that it is completely crazy. If we read it, it does not make any sense. Well, maybe the beginning and end make sense, but everything in the middle sounds like a sophisticated form of nonsense, which can be said to be the basic feature of the *Prajnaparamita Sutras* in general. If we like the word "no," we might like the sutra because that is the main word it uses—no this, no that, no everything. We could also say that it is a sutra about wisdom, but it is a sutra about crazy wisdom. When we read it, it sounds nuts, but that is actually where the wisdom part comes in. What the *Heart Sutra* (like all *Prajnaparamita Sutras*) does is to cut through, deconstruct, and demolish all our usual conceptual frameworks, all our rigid ideas, all our belief systems, all our reference points, including any with regard to our spiritual path. It does so on a very fundamental level, not just in terms of thinking and concepts, but also in terms of our perception, how we see the world, how we hear, how we smell, taste, touch, how we regard and emotionally react to ourselves and others, and so on. This sutra pulls the rug out from underneath our feet and does not leave anything intact that we can think of, nor even a lot of things that we cannot think of. This is called "crazy wisdom." I guess I should give you a warning here that this sutra is hazardous to your samsaric sanity. What Sangharakshita says about the *Diamond Sutra* equally applies to all *Prajnaparamita Sutras*, including the *Heart Sutra*:

> If we insist that the requirements of the logical mind be satisfied, we are missing the point. What the *Diamond Sutra* is actually delivering is not a systematic treatise, but a series of sledgehammer blows, attacking from this side and that, to try and break through our fundamental delusion. It is not going to make things easy for the logical mind by putting

things in a logical form. This sutra is going to be confusing, irritating, annoying, and unsatisfying—and perhaps we cannot ask for it to be otherwise. If it were all set forth neatly and clearly, leaving no loose ends, we might be in danger of thinking we had grasped the Perfection of Wisdom.

—SANGHARAKSHITA, *Wisdom beyond Words*

We could say that the *Heart Sutra* is like a big koan. But it is not just *one* koan, it is like those Russian dolls: there is one big doll on the outside and then there is a smaller one inside that first one, and there are many more smaller ones in each following one. Likewise, all the "nos" in the big koan of the sutra are little koans. Every little phrase with a "no" is a different koan in terms of what the "no" relates to, such as "no eye," "no ear," and so on. It is an invitation to contemplate what that means. "No eye," "no ear" sounds very simple and very straightforward, but if we go into the details, it is not that straightforward at all. In other words, all those different "no" phrases give us different angles or facets of the main theme of the sutra, which is emptiness. Emptiness means that things do not exist as they seem, but are like illusions and like dreams. They do not have a nature or a findable core of their own. Each one of those phrases makes us look at that very same message. The message or the looking are not really different, but we look at it in relation to different things. What does it mean that the eye is empty? What does it mean that visible form is empty? What does it mean that even wisdom, buddhahood, and nirvana are empty?

From an ordinary Buddhist point of view, we could even say that the *Heart Sutra* is not only crazy, but it is iconoclastic or even heretical. Many people have complained about the *Prajnaparamita Sutras* because they also trash all the hallmarks of Buddhism itself, such as the four noble truths, the Buddhist path, and nirvana. These sutras not only say that our ordinary thoughts, emotions, and perceptions are invalid and that they do not really exist as they seem to, but that the same goes for all the concepts and frameworks of philosophical schools—non-Buddhist schools, Buddhist schools, and even the Mahayana, the tradition to which the *Prajnaparamita Sutras* belong. Is there any other spiritual tradition that says, "Everything that we teach, just forget about it"? It is somewhat similar to the boss of Microsoft having publicly recommended that PC users should not buy Windows Vista anymore, but instead go straight from Windows XP to Windows 7. Basically he was advertising against his own product.

The *Heart Sutra* is similar to that, except that it tells us only what not to buy, but not what to buy instead.

In brief, if we have never seen the *Heart Sutra* and we read it, it sounds crazy because it just keeps saying "no, no, no." If we are trained in Buddhism, it also sounds crazy (maybe even more so) because it negates everything that we have learned and try to cultivate.

The *Heart Sutra* and the other *Prajnaparamita Sutras* talk about a lot of things, but their most fundamental theme is the basic groundlessness of our experience. They say that no matter what we do, no matter what we say, and no matter what we feel, we need not believe any of it. There is nothing whatsoever to hold on to, and even that is not sure. So these sutras pull the rug out from under us all the time and take away all our favorite toys. Usually when someone takes away one of our mental toys, we just find new toys. That is one of the reasons why many of the *Prajnaparamita Sutras* are so long—they list all the toys we can think of and even more, but our mind still keeps grasping at new ones. The basic point is to get to a place where we actually stop searching for and grasping at the next toy. Then we need to see how *that* state of mind feels. How does our mind feel when we are not grasping at anything, when we are not trying to entertain ourselves, and when our mind is not going outside (or not going anywhere at all), when there is no place left to go?

Usually we think that if a given phenomenon is not something, it must be nothing, and if it is not nothing, it must be something. But emptiness is just a word for pointing out the fact that no matter what we say or think about something, it does not really correctly characterize that something because our dualistic mind just gets stuck in one extreme or the other. Thus, we could say that emptiness is like thinking outside of the box—that is, the box of black-and-white thinking or dualistic thinking. As long as we stay within the ballpark of dualistic thinking, there is always existence, nonexistence, permanence, extinction, good, and bad. Within that frame of reference, we will never get beyond it, no matter if we are religious, a scientist, a Buddhist, an agnostic, or whatever. Emptiness tells us that we have to step out of that ballpark altogether. Emptiness points to the most radical transformation of our entire outlook with regard to ourselves and the world. Emptiness not only means the end of the world as we know it, but that this world never really existed in the first place.

Why is it called the *Heart Sutra*? It has that name because it teaches the heart of the Mahayana, primarily in terms of the view. However, the basic motivation of the Mahayana is also implicitly contained in this sutra in the form of Avalokiteshvara, the great bodhisattva who is the embodiment of the loving-kindness and compassion of all buddhas. It is actually the only *Prajnaparamita Sutra* in which Avalokiteshvara appears at all, and in it he is even the main speaker. Thus, the *Heart Sutra* teaches emptiness through the epitome of compassion. It is often said that, in a sense, emptiness is the heart of the Mahayana, but the heart of emptiness is compassion. The scriptures even use the phrase "emptiness with a heart of compassion." It is crucial to never forget that. The main reason for Avalokiteshvara's presence here is to symbolize the aspect of compassion and to emphasize that we should not miss out on it. If we just read all the "nos" and then get hooked on the "no path" of "no self" and "no attainment," it gets a little dreary or depressing and we may wonder, "Why are we doing this?" or "Why are we not doing this?" In fact, the heart essence of the *Prajnaparamita* teachings and the Mahayana is the union of emptiness and compassion. If we look at the larger *Prajnaparamita Sutras*, we see that they teach both aspects extensively. In addition to teaching about emptiness, they also speak about the path in great detail, such as how to cultivate loving-kindness and compassion, how to do certain meditations, and how to progress through the paths. They do not always say "no," but also sometimes present things in a more positive light. Even the *Heart Sutra*, toward the end, comes up with a few phrases without "no."

Without developing a soft heart and compassion, which like water softens our mental rigidity, there is a danger that the teachings on emptiness can make our hearts even harder. If we think we understand emptiness, but our compassion does not increase, or even lessens, we are on the wrong track. Therefore, for those of us who are Buddhists, it is good and necessary to give rise to compassion and bodhichitta before we study, recite, and contemplate this sutra. All others may connect with any spot of compassion that they can find in their hearts.

In yet another way, we could say that the *Heart Sutra* is an invitation to just let go and relax. We can replace all the words in this sutra that go with "no," such as "no eye," "no ear," with all our problems, such as "no depression," "no fear," "no unemployment," "no war," and so on. That might sound simplistic, but if we do that and actually make it into a contemplation on what all those things such as depression, fear, war, and economic crisis actually are, it can become very powerful, maybe even more powerful than the original words in the sutra. Usually we are not that interested in, for example, our ears and whether they really exist or not, so with regard to contemplating what emptiness means, one of the basic principles of the *Prajnaparamita Sutras* is to make the examination as personal as possible. It is not about reciting some stereotypical formula or the *Heart Sutra* without ever getting to the core of our own clinging to real existence with regard to those phenomena to which we obviously do cling, or our own ego-clinging. For example, the *Heart Sutra* does not say "no self," "no home," "no partner," "no job," "no money," which are the things we usually care about. Therefore, in order to make it more relevant to our life, we have to fill those in. The *Heart Sutra* gives us a basic template of how to contemplate emptiness, but the larger *Prajnaparamita Sutras* fill in a lot of stuff, not only saying "no eye," "no ear," and so on. They go through endless lists of all kinds of phenomena, so we are welcome to come up with our own personal lists of phenomena that map out our personal universe and then apply the approach of the *Heart Sutra* to those lists.

There are accounts in several of the larger *Prajnaparamita Sutras* about people being present in the audience who had already attained certain advanced levels of spiritual development or insight that liberated them from samsaric existence and suffering. These people, who are called "arhats" in Buddhism, were listening to the Buddha speaking about emptiness and then had different reactions. Some thought, "This is crazy, let's go," and left. Others stayed, but some of them had heart attacks, vomited blood, and died. It seems they didn't leave in time. These arhats were so shocked by what they were hearing that they died on the spot. That's why somebody suggested to me that we could call the *Heart Sutra* the *Heart Attack Sutra*. Another meaning of that could be that this sutra goes right for the heart of the matter, while mercilessly attacking all ego trips that prevent us from waking up to our true heart. In any case, so far nobody has had a heart attack here, which is good news. But the bad news is that probably nobody understood it either.

Uprooting the Seeds of Anger

Jules Shuzen Harris

There is little that causes more suffering in this world than anger—our own and others. Yet as Zen teacher Jules Shuzen Harris, Sensei, tells us, anger has something to teach us. Do we have the courage to listen?

We operate under a common illusion that the things that make us angry lie outside of ourselves, that they are external to us. Something out there is in opposition to our need for safety and security; it threatens our comfort or position. We feel a need to defend our vulnerable selves. Anger limits us. But if we have the courage to look at our anger and its causes and to learn from it, we can develop an open heart—a heart of genuine compassion.

My own journey in dealing with anger has included work with several systems of martial arts. Initially I studied the martial arts to learn how to defend against the enemy outside myself, which I thought was the reason for my anger. After some time, I was drawn to *iaido*, the art of drawing, cutting with, and sheathing a Samurai sword. Loosely translated, the term *iaido* means being able to fit into any situation harmoniously. Unlike many other martial art forms, *iaido* is noncombative, which was key: to create a harmonious relationship with myself, I had to confront the enemy within—and the enemy was my own anger.

I have often observed that while we each experience anger in our own way, a more general sense of anger pervades our society. That is, as a culture, we are angry. Our sense of humor is very sarcastic. A lot of what we find entertaining involves putting someone down. We have slapstick comedy: people running around doing mean, spiteful things that we are supposed to find funny. Whether it is a television show or a new viral Internet video, we find humor in words that mock or put others down, or insults that allow us to watch from the outside as someone else is subjected to some form of humiliation. We might ask ourselves, "What's funny about that?" Not much. Laughing at others' misfortune is a kind of expression of our own anger.

Have we ever said to someone, "You're lazy," or "You're a bitch," or "You're an insufferable bastard"? Of course. We've all done that in one way or another. Or maybe we have said, "If it weren't for you, I would be better off," or "It's because of you that I am suffering." It is as if we believe that by putting others down, by placing the blame or responsibility for our unhappiness on others, we can make ourselves better or relieve our own feelings of inadequacy. But anger doesn't make us feel better. As Chögyam Trungpa Rinpoche said, "You cannot really eliminate pain through aggression. The more you kill, the more you strengthen the killer who will create new things to be killed. The aggression grows until finally there is no space; the whole environment has been solidified."

Among the three poisons we find the Pali term *dosa*, "anger." The three poisons of anger, greed, and delusion keep us in bondage and control us—they overwhelm our best intentions and cause us to do harm to others. We may even cause the greatest hurt to the people we most care about. We don't want to hurt them, or ourselves, but we are driven by our anger. Many times we find that a feeling that arises in us is the outward manifestation of a deeper underlying emotion or experience. We might explore this possibility by asking ourselves about where our anger really comes from. What is the other side of anger? Fear. We can't free ourselves until we work through both our anger and our fear. And what is the cause of fear? Ultimately, it is the fear of nonexistence, death, the fear of losing ourselves and being forgotten. But a fear of death translates into a fear of living, because impermanence is itself a fundamental condition of our lives. In this fear lie the seeds of anger.

How do we break the cycle of anger? We all know anger from experience, but when we are asked to pause and consider, "What is this anger?" it's not always so easy to see what it is. Yet when we approach our feelings of anger with awareness, with mindfulness, it becomes a productive part of our practice. We find, after all, that anger has something to teach us.

Anger is what Thich Nhat Hanh calls "habit energy." Like most habits, it takes just one particular event or word or incident to trigger us, as quick as a snap of the fingers. Just because we have a *kensho* experience and see into our true nature and maybe for a second or two experience some sense of bliss, that doesn't mean that we won't return to habit energy five minutes or an hour later. If someone does something that irritates you, ask yourself the question, "Who is it that is ticked off? Who is it that's angry?" We'll find that there is no self to get angry or to defend.

And yet there may be something that sets us off again and again, as reliably as an alarm clock. Maybe we know what some of those things are. Often other people can tell us what brings out our flashes of anger even if we are not ourselves aware of them. But these habitual flashpoints offer us an opportunity to see ourselves more deeply, with a fuller understanding and with greater compassion, to look at what incited our angry reaction, and to follow the thread within ourselves. All we need is the space between trigger and reaction to mindfully look within.

So where do we find this space to separate ourselves from our anger? Many Buddhist traditions teach that all things are insubstantial. When we see this, we see that the support for anger and hate is eroded and eventually destroyed. This speaks to one of the three marks of existence—impermanence. We have all found ourselves in situations that illustrate the transitory nature of events. Something happens to us that makes us angry; perhaps we get into an argument at home with a partner at the very start of the day. A couple of hours later, we're at work and we're still thinking about the incident. More time goes by, and we continue to stew over it at lunchtime, and by the time we get home, we're still holding on to it. But where is it? Where is the incident? It's like last night's supper—it doesn't exist.

Over and over again, I tell students dealing with anger, "This practice is about being mindful!" While that may sound simple, it is in fact a very, very difficult practice because it goes against a lot of what we hold sacred. Many of us have a particular group of gods that we worship. It's not God, Jesus, or Buddha. We worship pleasure, comfort, and security. Despite knowing that everything is impermanent, we still hold on to objects that we think will bring us security. We cling to what we believe will spare us from discomfort, and when these things slip out of our grasp, fear and anger arise.

Part of mindfulness is looking at our reactions and perceptions—if we are all truly one body, why are we cutting off the relationship with our partner, our coworker, or our friend? If my hand is in pain, do I cut it off? Of course not. I take care of it. I take some Tylenol. I look more carefully into what might be causing the pain—maybe it's an injury, or it could be that I'm developing arthritis and need to think of some therapies. But when it comes to anger, we cut ourselves off because we have an investment in maintaining who we think we are. Anger limits our expression of seeing our whole self. As a divisive force, it prevents us from living a fully rich life of connectedness. Instead of experiencing the one body that pervades everywhere, anger isolates us and reinforces the sense of a separate self, preventing us from identifying with and feeling compassion for others.

Mindfulness is cultivated through meditation practice. That is one of the reasons why I like the focused practice period of *sesshin*, several days of intensive sitting. It is amazing how much stuff surfaces in sesshin. In my first few years practicing Zen, I thought of myself as a pretty laid-back, easygoing guy. But then during these intensive meditation periods, I couldn't believe the amount of anger and rage that came up. I was ready to kill the teacher, kill the monks, and burn down the monastery! It stood in stark contrast to my ideas of who I thought I was. My anger was exacerbated by having the duty of scrubbing the toilets with a toothbrush. But all along the way, I continued meditating. And at some point, scrubbing the toilet with a toothbrush became a practice of mindfulness for me.

When we work with anger in Buddhist practice, we work with it a little differently than you would in psychotherapy. We don't ask you to beat a pillow, open the window, and scream. When I was a psychotherapist, I had a Bozo the Clown bop bag in my office; you could hit it and it would just bounce back. And I would say, "Just keep pounding it, get it all out!" But that's not our approach. In Buddhism, we work to illuminate the fundamental truth of our self-nature. When anger arises, it is pointing to something. Our anger is a clue to our underlying beliefs about ourselves. It can help to reveal our constructed sense of self-identity.

Today many psychotherapists embrace Buddhist practice as a way of looking at ourselves in relationship to others. The Identity System developed by Stanley Block, MD, involves two processes called "mind-body mapping" and "bridging." Mind-body mapping as a part of Buddhist practice requires an openness to adapting the dharma for a particular time, place, and person—in this case for the Western psyche. You begin mind-body mapping by paying attention to a particular thought that is on your mind, perhaps one that is connected to strong feelings. Then, using this first thought as a focal point, you trace the paths of further thoughts and ideas that are generated out of the initial thought. At the same time, you give attention to how your thoughts feel in relationship to the body. We all have personal requirements, thoughts, or rules about how we—and the world—should be. While they may remain hidden from our conscious awareness, we can recognize them by our anger, which arises when our requirements are broken. By deepening our ability to be fully present, we have a better chance of seeing our requirements and letting them go, uprooting the seeds that sprout into anger.

This exploration, together with an approach called "bridging," has proven to be a valuable tool. Bridging is akin to mindfulness. When you are washing the dishes, you are focused on touch, the place, the water on your hands, the feel of the sponge; or when you are driving your car, you listen to the hum of the engine, the vibration of your hands on the steering wheel. Bridging and mind-body mapping help us deal with the shadow beliefs we carry with us—"I'm not good enough," "I'm undeserving"—that create negative story lines. Our anger can be seen as a defense against these vulnerable feelings and negative self-beliefs. The deep-seated fear and anger we harbor has to do with our feelings of a damaged self. Mind-body mapping and bridging enable practitioners to see how they create their suffering in relationship to the body rather than a situation outside themselves. From a Buddhist perspective, we are trying to reach the place where there is no separation, no subject, no object. Bringing our mind back again and again to a place of present-moment awareness, we create a space where we let go of our habitual reaction patterns and our recurring negative feelings. We then open the opportunity to view ourselves—and others—with real compassion.

Our meditation practice is also a place where we can work directly with our experience of anger by becoming the anger. To "become the anger" does not mean to act it out. It means we stop separating ourselves from it; we experience it fully so that we can understand what's behind it. In sitting zazen, we can encourage the anger to come up. We become intimate with anger, and in doing so, we watch it dissipate.

We have to look deeply into the cause of our suffering. Our anger not only creates suffering for others, but it also creates more suffering for us. We might take a mind-body perspective that what we think affects every cell in our body. Neuroscientists suggest that our neurons are affected by our immediate environment. If we are in a hostile, argumentative, negative environment, then that affects our neural networks and neurochemistry, and our nervous system becomes conditioned to react every time we go into that environment. So we could say that very environment becomes toxic. We've all had the experience of walking into a certain space and feeling at home, and going into a different space and becoming very agitated or depressed, because of the subtle energy or our unconscious relationship to the place.

We must remember that we create our own anger. No one makes it for us. If we move from a particular event directly to our reaction, we are skipping a crucial awareness, a higher perspective on our own reactivity. What is that middle step, that deeper awareness? It is mindfulness about our own beliefs, our attitude, our understanding or lack of understanding about what has really happened. We notice that a given situation reliably provokes our anger, and yet somebody else can be exposed to the very same situation and not react angrily. Why is that? No one can tell us: we each have to find the answer ourselves, and to do that, we need to give ourselves the space to reflect mindfully.

We're going to keep getting angry. It's going to come up. It has come up in our lives before, and it will come up again. This practice is about becoming more mindful, becoming aware of how we are getting stuck. With care and work, we find ways to get unstuck. But we also know that the moment we get unstuck, we're going to get stuck again. That's why it is called a practice—we never arrive. So when you find yourself upset or angry, use the moment as a part of your practice, as an opportunity to notice and uproot the seeds of anger and move into the heart of genuine compassion.

I Kinda Vow

Genine Lentine

Zen practitioners traditionally renew their vows in a monthly ritual called the "full moon ceremony." Those precepts are pretty hard to keep strictly, considering where most of us really are on the spiritual path. So the Zen practitioner Genine Lentine has written a humorous but perhaps more realistic set of vows she calls the "half moon ceremony."

ALL:

> Half my ancient twisted karma
> From well-nigh beginningless greed, hate, and delusion,
> Born through body, speech, and mind
> I now kind of avow.

GRAVE PRECEPTS

[Doshi reads each vow, and the assembly recites the vow in response]

One

> *I vow not to kill.*
> Well, except when it comes to some very small,
> very icky, perhaps sentient, but nevertheless very icky,
> very tiny, very numerous beings, beings who walk on food
>   surfaces,

or crawl on my skin, especially those beings whose bites line up
    in threes—
I made the mistake of googling these beings
I mean, have you seen pictures of those beings on the Internet?
Here, I'll show you, do you want to look at some now?

Two

I vow not to take what is not given,
but just to borrow it, or only take it if I think
the person who owns it would have said, take it
if they'd been there, or if they had so much
they'd never notice the little bit I took.
Okay, also, I should say in A.M. service, I have stolen glances.
I have held my gaze well above 45 degrees.
I have, in fact, held my gaze at 60 or even 70 degrees,
I have, I will tell you, held such a glance
far longer than would be required
for finding my place in a row.
Using service to check people out
is decidedly less than wholesome
but some people do look mad hot in their robes.

Three

I vow not to misuse sexuality?
Um, misuse sexuality? Trust me,
you won't find me misusing anything,
if you know what I mean. Ask anyone.
But okay, I'm giving the six-month rule a spin.
Six days is more like it, but I'm doing my best.
I tell myself: Penetration—only that of wisdom,
only that of realization, like a long summer rain,
that kind of warm august rain
when you're out walking barefoot in grass,
and the air is just shy of liquid,

and the mist is so fine, and so deep, and so slow,
you don't even notice you're wet
until you're soaked, until your white dress,
your very thin, very sheer, white dress
is just drenched and clings to your body.
I ask myself, When the dharma soaks your dress
Can you then ever really take such a dress off?
I say to myself: Arousal—only that of the bodhi-mind.
But sometimes, nothing more than a shadow
passing through my own, cast onto the zendo wall,
can bring on a shudder—or a sleeve brushing my bare arm,
or in a very quiet zendo, the sound of a certain person's
        breathing,
is quite more than enough, so maybe after all,
six months won't be so long.

Four

I vow to refrain from false speech.
Speech is just too potent and precious to be reckless with it.
        L.O.L.
Thus, I would never, under any circumstance, tilt the truth,
even a little, and especially, not on the tenken pad.

Five

I totally vow to refrain from abusing intoxicants.
Seriously. I mean, abuse this excellent bud?
That would just be wrong.
Plus, Dude, is using it when I need it, abusing it?
Have you ever had super harsh insomnia?
Also my back is whacked, I got a card.
I keep it chill. I don't overdo it.
Like when Luke and me were driving out to Mad River Beach?
and he just totally cashed the bowl,
vacuumed it, did not hand it to me once,

and I'm like, Dude!
and he's like, What?
Fire up another one, he says,
and so I pull off of Old Arcata Road,
and as the wheels turn onto the gravel it's just freakin' weird
because my favorite song is on
and it's right at that point, you know
where Kurt says, a mosquito, my libido,
the most awesome part of the most awesome song,
and at that exact moment this huge deer leaps out
right in front of the car and Luke is like, Dude!
You almost killed that buck. And right then I was just all like,
I haven't had one hit off that bowl
and I'm just feeling how precious everything is
and this hum, like, my legs, are shaking
and these rays of light just, I kid you not, pour out of my body,
and Luke's looking out the front window,
and he's all, This is my mom's truck, J, watch your driving,
and I'm like, Friend, Friend, Friend, you know I love your
       mother.
And he's all, I'm sorry man,
and I'm all, No worries,
and—Wait, wait, wait, what was the question?

Six

I vow not to slander, but to gossip mindfully about juicy tidbits.
Granted, haphazard talk is corrosive,
But once in the gaitan, I was standing behind a person,
—I won't say his name here now—
and he stepped into the zendo with the foot
farthest away from the doorframe,
and I raised this with my practice leader, and with his,
complained about it to my roommate, and we both rolled
       our eyes
as if to say, of course,

and in small group I brought it up without mentioning his
    name.
I was just trying to help his practice, but I would be lying
if I didn't say it was also because this guy
really works my nerve.

Seven

I vow not to praise self at the expense of others.
If only other people would follow my example on this!
Oh this one's very up for me right now in my practice.
I've been practicing with this one a lot recently.
Not praising self at the expense of others. It's a big one,
but you know I take it as an opportunity
to really look and see what's going on for me.
What's coming up for me at the moment around this,
in my interactions with others,
is how when my needs aren't being met,
and I make a request, and it's simply not heard,
instead of just being able to take this up with the person,
what I'll usually do is take it on and make it my own problem,
but then I'll just vent with my partner about the whole thing.
I'm really looking at this closely and practicing with it,
seeing, what if I just try asking for what I need with the person.
And then another thing I noticed when I looked at it
is that I'm more likely to praise others at the expense of self.
I was telling my friend from outside about this
but she couldn't hear what I was saying.
She doesn't understand things like I do.
But then, she hasn't been practicing as long as I have.

Eight

I vow not to be avaricious.
That's why if there are only three cookies
in the small kitchen, I figure it isn't enough
for everyone, so I think in such a case, isn't it better

if I just have them myself
so no one else will suffer from wanting them?

Nine

I'm all about not harboring ill will.
It's fine, really. It's not a problem.
I accept it. Some. things. you. just. have to. let. go.

Ten

I vow not to abuse the Three Treasures.
Sure, I'm basically on board with this one.
Abuse sex, I get it. Abuse drugs, okay.
But how do you abuse the Three Treasures?
Am I missing something?
Should I try it once just to know what I'm giving up?
I'm not totally clear on what I'm actually vowing to do
or um, not do, but come on, I'm all for it.
I mean, what I'm all for, is not abusing them.
It's the Three Treasures we're talking about!
Count me in, I mean, or out, you know, of abusing them,
but for sure, I vow not to abuse The Three Treasures,
whatever that means.

DEDICATION

Thus on this half-moon midafternoon,
at this time that is otherwise perfect for napping,
though we cannot yet see the moon in its fullness,
we know it is there, in the shadow,
we're at least pretty sure it's there—
let's say we can go to the bank on its being there,
somewhere—
Let us, thus, this afternoon, tolerate the broken,
the irregular, the flawed, the not so swift,

the not nearly quite all there yet, the best guess,
that which we just barely manage to muster, the
      half-asterisked,
through all world systems, to the unborn nature of all being.

Contributors

REB ANDERSON is a lineage holder in the Soto Zen tradition and a former abbot of the San Francisco Zen Center. In 1970 he was ordained as a Zen priest by Shunryu Suzuki Roshi, who gave him the name Tenshin Zenki (meaning "naturally real; the whole works"), and he received dharma transmission in 1983. Anderson is the author of *Warm Smiles from Cold Mountains*, *Being Upright*, and *The Third Turning of the Wheel*, excerpted here. He continues to teach at Zen Center and lives with his family at Green Gulch Farm.

EZRA BAYDA was initially trained in the Gurdjieff tradition and began practicing Zen meditation in 1970. He lives and teaches at Zen Center San Diego and is the author of five books: *Being Zen*, *At Home in the Muddy Water*, *Saying Yes to Life (Even the Hard Parts)*, *Zen Heart*, and, most recently, *Beyond Happiness: The Zen Way to True Contentment*.

SYLVIA BOORSTEIN is one of American Buddhism's most popular teachers. Through her personal teachings and best-selling books, including *Happiness Is an Inside Job*, *Pay Attention, for Goodness' Sake*, and *It's Easier Than You Think*, she has taught accessible but authentic dharma and touched the lives of many thousands. She is a PhD psychotherapist and a cofounding teacher of Spirit Rock Meditation Center in Woodacre, California.

KARL BRUNNHÖLZL is a senior teacher in the Nalandabodhi community of Dzogchen Ponlop Rinpoche and was recently bestowed the title of *khenpo*. He is a physician and studied Tibetology and Sanskrit at the University of Hamburg, Germany. He is the author and translator of numerous texts, including *Luminous Heart*, *Gone Beyond*, *Groundless Paths*, and *The Heart Attack Sutra*, excerpted in this anthology.

Through her powerful teachings, best-selling books, and retreats attended by thousands, PEMA CHÖDRÖN has become today's most important American-born teacher of Buddhism. In books such as *The Wisdom of No Escape*, *The Places That Scare You*, and *Living Beautifully with Uncertainty and Change*, excerpted here, she has helped hundreds of thousands of people discover how life's challenges can become opportunities for awakening. Pema Chödrön received full ordination as a Buddhist nun in 1981, and as resident teacher at Gampo Abbey in Cape Breton, Nova Scotia, she has dedicated herself to establishing a genuine monastic tradition in the West.

ZOKETSU NORMAN FISCHER is a writer, poet, and Zen Buddhist teacher. He served as co-abbot of San Francisco Zen Center from 1995 to 2000 and is the founder and spiritual director of the Everyday Zen Foundation, an organization dedicated to adapting Zen Buddhist teachings to Western culture. His books include *Opening to You: Zen-Inspired Translations of the Psalms*, *Taking Our Places: The Buddhist Path to Truly Growing Up*, and *Training in Compassion: Zen Teachings on the Practice of Lojong*.

JAMES ISHMAEL FORD is a guiding teacher of Boundless Way Zen and a Unitarian Universalist minister. He is the author of *Zen Master Who? A Guide to the People and Stories of Zen* and coeditor of *The Book of Mu: Essential Writings on Zen's Most Important Koan*. His newest book is *If You're Lucky, Your Heart Will Break: Field Notes from a Zen Life*, excerpted here.

BONNIE FRIEDMAN is the author of *The Thief of Happiness* and *Writing Past Dark: Envy, Fear, Distraction, and Other Dilemmas in the Writer's Life*. She is currently assistant professor in the creative writing program at the University of North Texas. She has published frequently in the *New York Times*, and her work has appeared in *O*, *Redbook*, *Self*, the *Ladies Home Journal*, and many literary journals. She divides her time between Brooklyn, New York, and Denton, Texas.

NATALIE GOLDBERG is one of American Buddhism's best-known writers. She is the author of the classic *Writing Down the Bones: Freeing the Writer Within*, and has been teaching seminars on writing as a practice for the last thirty years. Among her many best-selling books are *Old Friend from Far Away*, *The Great Failure*, and the 2013 volume *The True Secret of Writing*. In *Living Color: A Writer Paints Her World*, she writes about her second creative practice as a painter.

JOSEPH GOLDSTEIN first became interested in Buddhism as a Peace Corps volunteer in Thailand in 1965, and he has been leading insight and loving-kindness meditation retreats worldwide since 1974. He is a cofounder of the Insight Meditation Society in Barre, Massachusetts, where he is one of the organization's guiding teachers, and in 1989 he helped establish the Barre Center for Buddhist Studies. His books include *A Heart Full of Peace*, *Insight Meditation: The Practice of Freedom*, and *One Dharma: The Emerging Western Buddhism*.

JULES SHUZEN HARRIS is a Soto Zen priest and the founder of Soji Zen Center in Lansdowne, Pennsylvania. He holds an EdD with a concentration in applied human development, and as a psychotherapist he has found creative ways to synthesize Western psychology and Zen. Harris also focuses on the relationship between Zen and the martial arts. He holds black belts in *iaido* (the art of drawing and cutting with a samurai sword) and *kendo* (Japanese fencing) and has founded Japanese swordsmanship schools in Albany and Salt Lake City.

PICO IYER is an essayist, travel writer, and novelist whose writing often addresses the theme of cultural identity in a global age. His books include *The Global Soul, Sun after Dark, The Open Road: The Global Journey of the Fourteenth Dalai Lama* (the result of his more than thirty years of talks and travels with His Holiness), and *The Man within My Head*, a reflection on how to mix kindness with realism.

Dzongsar Jamyang Khyentse Rinpoche was born in Bhutan and recognized as the main incarnation of the Khyentse lineage of Tibetan Buddhism. He supervises his traditional seat of Dzongsar Monastery in Eastern Tibet and Buddhist colleges in India and Bhutan. He has founded three nonprofit organizations and established Buddhist centers in Australia, North America, and the Far East. He is the author of *What Makes You Not a Buddhist* and *Not for Happiness*, excerpted in this anthology. Under the name Khyentse Norbu, he has directed the acclaimed films *The Cup* and *Travelers & Magicians*.

Kay Larson is an art critic, columnist, and frequent contributor to the *New York Times*. She began practicing Buddhism in the Zen tradition in 1994 and now practices in the Tibetan tradition at Karma Triyana Dharmachakra monastery in upstate New York. *Where the Heart Beats* is her first book. She says of writing it: "This book has been a fifteen-year journey into the world of John Cage, who was teacher to so many, and who taught me, too. Cage modeled a life that lives on in the daily moments of those who knew, loved, and were taught by him."

Genine Lentine is a poet and author of the chapbooks *Mr. Worthington's Beautiful Experiments on Splashes* and *Poses: An Essay Drawn from the Model*. She teaches an ongoing Sunday writing workshop at the San Francisco Zen Center, where she was recently artist-in-residence.

Judy Lief is a Buddhist teacher and the editor of the *Profound Treasury of the Ocean of Dharma*, a new three-volume series presenting the Hinayana, Mahayana, and Vajrayana Seminary teachings of the late Chögyam Trungpa Rinpoche. Lief has been teaching on the subject of lojong for more than thirty years and edited Trungpa Rinpoche's commentary on lojong, *Training the Mind and Cultivating Loving-Kindness*. The author of *Making Friends with Death*, Lief teaches a contemplative approach to facing death and working with the dying, and she leads an annual retreat for women touched by cancer titled "Courageous Women, Fearless Living."

KAREN MAEZEN MILLER is a Zen Buddhist priest and teacher at the Hazy Moon Zen Center in Los Angeles. She is the author of *Momma Zen* and *Hand Wash Cold: Care Instructions for an Ordinary Life*. She lives with her husband and daughter in Sierra Madre, California, where she has a century-old Japanese garden in the backyard and does a lot of weeding, raking, and picking up after the dog. "It helps me not take myself so seriously," she says.

SAKYONG MIPHAM RINPOCHE is the spiritual leader of Shambhala, an international network of meditation centers. He is the son of the late Chögyam Trungpa Rinpoche and was recognized as the incarnation of the great Tibetan teacher and scholar Mipham Jamyang Gyatso. He is the author of the best sellers *Ruling Your World*, *Turning the Mind into an Ally*, and *Running with the Mind of Meditation*, excerpted here. In addition to his position as Sakyong (Earth Protector) in the Shambhala tradition, he is a holder of the Kagyu and Nyingma lineages of Vajrayana Buddhism.

PHILLIP MOFFITT is director of the Life Balance Institute and a member of the Teachers' Council at Spirit Rock Meditation Center. He leads meditation retreats throughout the United States and Canada and teaches a weekly meditation class in Marin County, California. A former editor-in-chief of *Esquire* magazine, he is the author of *Dancing with Life* and *Emotional Chaos to Clarity: How to Live More Skillfully, Make Better Decisions, and Find Purpose in Life*, excerpted in this anthology.

RACHEL NEUMANN is the editorial director of Parallax Press, the publishing arm of Zen master Thich Nhat Hanh's community, and is the author of *Not Quite Nirvana: A Skeptic's Journey to Mindfulness*, excerpted here. She lives in the Bay Area and writes regularly on the intersections of mindfulness, parenting, politics, and the mess of daily life.

As a Zen master, poet, prolific author, and founder of the Engaged Buddhist movement, THICH NHAT HANH is one of the most renowned Buddhist teachers of our time. A social and antiwar activist in his native Vietnam, he was nominated for the Nobel Peace Prize in 1967 by Martin Luther King Jr. Still actively teaching in his eighties, Thich Nhat Hanh resides at practice centers in France and the United States and travels the world teaching the art of engaged and mindful living.

LODRO RINZLER is a practitioner and teacher in the Shambhala community. As a second-generation convert Buddhist, he began meditating as a child and sat retreats as a teenager, including a silent month-long retreat during which he shaved his head and took monastic robes and vows. His Buddhist advice column, "What Would Sid Do?" appears in the *Huffington Post* and on the website of the Interdependence Project each month. Rinzler writes from his apartment in New York City, which he shares with his dog, Tillie, and his cat, Justin Bieber.

DAVID RYNICK began formal Zen training in 1981 and was recognized in 2011 as a Zen master in the Korean Rinzai tradition. With his wife, the Zen teacher and writer Melissa Myozen Blacker, he leads the Boundless Way Temple in Worcester, Massachusetts, where he is also a member of the First Unitarian Church. *This Truth Never Fails: A Zen Memoir in Four Seasons*, excerpted here, is his first book. He is also a licensed sea kayak guide, novice jazz bass player, avid landscape gardener, and aspiring unicyclist.

ELIHU GENMYO SMITH began his Zen training in 1974 at the Zen Studies Society in New York and was ordained as a Buddhist priest in 1979. After completing formal koan study with Hakuyu Maezumi Roshi in 1984, he continued his training with Charlotte Joko Beck at Zen Center of San Diego. Genmyo is a cofounder of the Ordinary Mind Zen School and is resident teacher of the Prairie Zen Center in Champaign, Illinois. He is the author of *Ordinary Life, Wondrous Life* and *Everything Is the Way: Ordinary Mind Zen*, excerpted here.

IRA SUKRUNGRUANG is the author of the memoir *Talk Thai: The Adventures of Buddhist Boy*, and the coeditor of *What Are You Looking At? The First Fat Fiction Anthology* and *Scoot Over, Skinny: The Fat Nonfiction Anthology*.

SHYALPA TENZIN RINPOCHE is a meditation master and scholar in the Vajrayana Buddhist tradition. As spiritual guide of Shyalpa monastery and nunnery in Kathmandu, he guides over 130 monks and nuns in the Dzogchen Longchen Nyingtig tradition. Shyalpa Rinpoche is founder of the Tibetan Refugee Children's Fund, which to date has educated more than three hundred children from India and Nepal, and is head of Rangrig Yeshe, a nonprofit organization that organizes teachings and retreats throughout the United States. *Living Fully: Finding Joy in Every Breath*, excerpted here, is his first book.

For more than twenty years, TSOKNYI RINPOCHE has been teaching students worldwide about the innermost nature of mind as taught in the Tibetan Buddhist tradition. His lighthearted yet illuminating style appeals to beginners and advanced practitioners alike. Seeking a bridge between ancient wisdom and the modern mind, he has a keen interest in the ongoing dialogue between Western scientists and Buddhist practitioners. Tsoknyi Rinpoche is the author of three books: *Carefree Dignity*, *Fearless Simplicity*, and *Open Heart, Open Mind*, excerpted here.

Originally ordained in Japan as a monk in the Shingon tradition, SHINZEN YOUNG has undertaken extensive training in the Vajrayana, Zen, and Vipassana Buddhist traditions. He is known for his innovative application of mindfulness to pain management, recovery support, and psychotherapy. Young leads meditation retreats throughout North America and consults widely on meditation-related research in both the clinical and the basic science domains.

Credits

Reb Anderson, "The Third Turning of the Wheel." Adapted from *The Third Turning of the Wheel: Wisdom of the Samdhinirmocana Sutra*, by Reb Anderson, edited with a foreword by James William Coleman. © 2012 by Reb Anderson. Reprinted with permission of Rodmell Press. www.rodmellpress.com.

Ezra Bayda, "Breaking Through." From the Summer 2012 issue of *Tricycle: The Buddhist Review*.

Sylvia Boorstein, "The Three Marks of Existence." From the July 2012 issue of the *Shambhala Sun*.

Karl Brunnhölzl, "The Heart Attack Sutra." From *The Heart Attack Sutra*, by Karl Brunnhölzl. © 2012 by Karl Brunnhölzl. Reprinted by arrangement with Shambhala Publications, Inc., Boston, Massachusetts. www.shambhala.com.

Pema Chödrön, "Living Beautifully with Uncertainty and Change." From *Living Beautifully with Uncertainty and Change*, by Pema Chödrön. © 2012 by Pema Chödrön. Reprinted by arrangement with Shambhala Publications, Inc., Boston, Massachusetts. www.shambhala.com.

Norman Fischer, "Impermanence Is Buddha Nature." From the May 2012 issue of the *Shambhala Sun*.

James Ishmael Ford, "If You're Lucky, Your Heart Will Break." From *If You're Lucky, Your Heart Will Break: Field Notes from a Zen Life*, by James Ishmael Ford. © 2012 by James Ishmael Ford. Reprinted with permission from Wisdom Publications, 199 Elm Street, Somerville, Massachusetts 02144 U.S.A. www.wisdompubs.org.

Bonnie Friedman, "The Vagabond Queen of Craigslist." From the November 2012 issue of the *Shambhala Sun*.

Natalie Goldberg, "Waking Up to Happiness." From the July 2012 issue of the *Shambhala Sun*.

Joseph Goldstein, "Everyday Meditation: A Nine-Minute Daily Practice." From the Spring 2012 issue of *Tricycle: The Buddhist Review*. An earlier version of this teaching